POZAN

Based on a True Story
By JOHN CLARK

Do Aliens Exist?
Read and Judge
for Yourself

"POZAN"

By John Clark

POZAN

"I found it to be a fascinating account which stays close to what I know took place (as based upon our meetings over the years). John Clark is a brave and inquisitive man who has not only had a long series of bizarre personal encounters but has rejected the evil side for the good. His quest for closure and understanding is a model for many others."

Dr. Richard Haines
Retired NASA Scientist

"Great story. I find John Clark,s work most fascinating. What he reports is consonant with my findings with other subjects."

Dr. James A. Harder
Professor U. C. Berkeley.

"Pozan is eerily powerful."

Peter Brimelow
Senior Editor Forbes Magazine.

"A weird and wild ride that draws you in deeper and deeper as you gradually leave behind the known world and approach the supernatural. I tried to tell myself that this stuff only happens in the movies. That says it all."

Tim Randall
Georgetown University.

"A real page turner."

Cliff Garcia

TABLE OF CONTENTS

PROLOGUE

We were standing in front of the Washington Monument, when Tom asked me to go for a short ride with him. I told him that I didn't have much time before I had to meet my girlfriend back at the National Art Gallery, but he assured me it wouldn't take long. I decided it would be worth being a little late if I could finally get some answers after my nearly 20 year quest to do so.

We climbed into Tom's Ford Fairlane and drove about a half hour to somewhere near Potomac, Maryland. We pulled up in front of an unmarked, gated entrance, and, after Tom had a few words with the armed guard, we were allowed access to the property. As we approached the one-story building, I noticed it had very few windows. A garage door opened, and Tom drove inside. He parked, and we walked down a long, tiled hallway that had absolutely nothing on the walls. It was a very sterile atmosphere, reminding me of a hospital. When we came to an elevator, we stepped inside, and Tom punched a button. The elevator descended for several minutes, causing me to wonder just how far underground we had actually traveled. The doors opened, and we walked down another long corridor, until it ended at a wall of stainless steel doors. Tom inserted an identification card into an electronic device, which I had only seen done in the movies. This caused me some concern as to what in the world I was getting myself into. The doors opened, and, as we passed through them, I felt as though I was stepping into a freezer. The temperature felt like around 30 to 40 degrees. Tom turned on the lights, and there, in front of us, were about 20 tables covered with white sheets. We walked by a few of them before Tom stopped in front of one and asked me to take a look. He pulled back the sheet, but at first it didn't register with me what I was actually seeing.

Tom Jolie - Washington, D.C., May 1993

Chapter 1
The Camping Trip

In June of 1975, I went on a camping trip that would change my life forever. My family and I planned the trip with our neighbors, Ralph, Olivia and their two daughters, ages twelve and ten and a seven year old son. They were an African-American family, and we had all become very good friends during the nearly two years we'd known each other. Our destination was Lake Isabella, which I had flown over on one of my first solo cross country flights five years earlier. I had reveled in the beauty of the area and felt this would be a great spot to bring my family camping sometime. And now, here we were, getting packed up to spend some time on the shores of that beautiful lake.

The trip started out like any normal family outing. My family was filled with anticipation and piled into my Ford Mach 1 amidst all the various suitcases and other items we felt were necessary for such an excursion. I must admit that I was just a tad bit excited myself. Since there were nine of us, we decided to rent a trailer. Ralph agreed to do the towing, since he had an Oldsmobile, which was larger than my car and better equipped to do the job. We left Long Beach around 9 or 10 A.M., picked up the trailer and began the 120 mile drive to Lake Isabella. The kids kept themselves entertained by playing various games, such as counting cars, checking license plates, etc. There wasn't a cloud in the sky as we neared the Mojave Desert, and it was hot, with the temperature around 98 degrees. I made a point to keep an eye on the rearview mirror to make sure Ralph wasn't having any difficulty keeping up with us. We began our climb from the desert floor into the mountains and were pleasantly relieved by the cooler, 70 degree temperatures. Finally, we entered the valley, and the kids, whose patience had begun to wear thin, screamed with delight when they spotted Lake Isabella. We all agreed that it was truly a spectacular sight. We stopped at the ranger station to get directions to an available campsite. As we drove through the campground, we were quite surprised to find just how crowded it was and felt fortunate that we were able to get a spot! When we located our site, I parked the car and went over to help Ralph get the trailer backed in. It didn't take me long to figure out that he wasn't too adept at maneuvering it into that rather narrow spot, and he was more than happy to turn the chore over to me. Eventually the trailer was parked, and we began unloading all the necessary items, such as food, fishing poles, bait, etc. Our children, a son who was 8 and a daughter 7, were already heading toward the water, with our dog, Puffy, leading the way. They were shouting at me to hurry up and join them, and I was certainly as ready as they were to get into that refreshing looking water! I had worked up quite a sweat setting up camp and was looking forward to luxuriating in the unbelievably clear, greenish-blue water, while drinking in the beauty of the surroundings.

Since the lake water is runoff from the mountains, it was very cold, but it felt great. The current was quite strong, so I warned the kids to be careful and to keep an eye on Puffy. Being a Spitz Terrier, he was built close to the ground and could run like the wind, which meant he could disappear in the blink of an eye. I watched Ralph, who was very tall and wiry, running down the path toward the water. I had to chuckle, because he was wearing rather baggy, gaudy shorts, and, with those skinny legs of his, he reminded me of a chicken on the run. I asked my son to go up and get the fishing gear, and he was off in a flash, returning in record time with the poles and the worms we had purchased near home and brought along in a cooler to use as bait. He had me bait his hook, as he simply did not like handling the worms, and his sister thought the whole process was "pretty gross," too. While my son was trying his hand at fishing, I decided it might be a good time to get the air mattress and see if I could conquer the small rapids, so I went to blow it up. When I returned to the river, I saw my son looking very proud as he was reeling in a small trout. I tried to encourage him by commenting that it looked big enough to feed all nine of us. I guess he believed me, because he ran back to the trailer and gave it to his mom to fix for dinner. My daughter was on the air mattress going down the rapids and screaming with excitement, which made me decide that we really should do this more often. My job required so much traveling, that vacations were few and far between. Sometime later, my son made the announcement that it was time for dinner. Ralph must have been very hungry, because before my son finished the sentence, he was already back at camp. My daughter, on the other hand, was a different story. She absolutely did not want to get out of the water, but she finally did so when she realized that I meant business. I asked what was for dinner, and Olivia replied "fish, of course," but we really had a complete spread, which included chicken, hamburgers, hot dogs, baked beans, potato salad and watermelon, as well as the fish. We ate at the two picnic tables, which were located about ten feet from the trailer.

As we were eating dinner, my wife noticed that there were a lot of

2

birds overhead, but I had to inform her that they weren't birds. They were bats-
----hundreds of them. Ralph's daughter's eyes got huge, because she said she
was afraid they would get caught in her hair. I assured her that wouldn't happen, but that she'd better be careful, because they might bite her neck. I was
joking, of course, but the kids didn't find it very humorous, so I had to make it
very clear to them that bats only bite people in movies.

      Once it began to get dark, we had the children gather up some wood,
and we built a fire. They began begging for "smores", which consist of graham
crackers, marshmallows and chocolate, so Olivia asked them to get the ingredi-
ents from the trailer. I had never seen my kids so helpful, and I didn't understand what all the excitement was about until I tasted them. They really were
delicious, and from then on I was hooked on them, too! Finally, my wife
announced that it was bedtime, and, after many protests from the children and
some bribing from me about an early fishing trip in the morning, they finally
began to get settled in for the night.

      While our wives were getting the kids taken care of, Ralph and I were
trying to figure out where we were going to sleep. The trailer only slept six
adults in two sets of bunkbeds and one double bed, but the kids doubled up.
There wasn't room in the trailer for us, so we knew we were going to have to
sleep somewhere in the great outdoors. Since this was Ralph's first camping
adventure, it was my suggestion that we put our sleeping bags on the picnic
tables, rather than on the ground. Ralph thought that was a good idea, since he
wasn't keen on the idea of sharing his sleeping bag with a rattlesnake. Before
retiring for the night, the four of us sat around the fire, and I began telling
some of my jokes. After about the second joke, everyone feigned exhaustion,
and we put out the fire and went to bed. Once Ralph and I got situated in our
sleeping bags, we both could tell that it was going to be a long night on those
hard, uncomfortable benches. I asked him if he would like to hear another
joke, and he said "Goodnight John." Tough crowd, I thought to myself. As I
was lying awake on the hard bench, I noticed what a nice clear night it was,
with the stars and the moon all looking incredibly bright in the cloudless sky,
and then I must have drifted off to sleep.

Chapter 2
The Encounter

I awakened to Ralph shouting, and Puffy, who was tied to a tree next to the picnic tables we were on, was barking and straining at the leash. As I sat up, I saw what I thought was a very tall person with long blonde hair. However, it didn't take me long at all to realize that it certainly wasn't any type of human I had ever seen. It wasn't making up and down movements like someone walking; instead, it was more like it was gliding. All I could see was the profile, but yet, somehow it was looking at me. It was just so difficult for me to believe my eyes, but I couldn't see a face on the creature. How could this possibly be true? Ralph kept asking me what it was, and I replied in a whisper that I had absolutely no idea, but that I sure wished it would go away. Puffy was going crazy, and it looked like he might break the leash at any minute, which also had me very concerned. Then the creature seemed to disappear, so Ralph got up and started walking toward the trailer, but then I realized he was heading for the car instead. I went over, picked up Puffy and hightailed it for the trailer. Olivia already had the door open, and she wanted to know what all the commotion was about, but before giving her an answer, I put Puffy down and reached under a bed for my brother's rifle that I had hidden there. It was a Russian AK 44 he had brought from Viet Nam and loaned to me for the trip. Olivia wanted to know where Ralph was, and when I told her he was in the car, she wanted to know what he was doing there. I told her I didn't know, but that I wanted her to please close the door. She started to argue about Ralph, but I assured her that he would be fine out there. I sat down in front of the door with the rifle aimed and ready. This upset Olivia terribly, because she thought I might accidentally shoot Ralph, and she pleaded with me to put the rifle down. I told her I had no intention of shooting Ralph, but that if anything else opened the door, I would shoot first and ask questions later. I was truly terrified and felt I had to be prepared to protect all of us, and yet, at the same time, I had to make the women and children feel that everything was under control by appearing to be calm.

I sat with my rifle pointed toward the door for the next three hours, and my muscles were aching all over my body. As soon as it started to get light out, I cautiously opened the door and was very much relieved to see that nothing was out there. I stepped out, with my eyes darting in every direction as I went over to the car to see how Ralph was doing. I noticed that he was asleep and had locked the doors. It only took one knock on the window, however, to awaken him, and he slowly rolled the window down. "Is it gone?" he whispered. "I think so.", and I decided to take a look around the area where we had seen the "thing." The ground was soft, so I began looking for tracks, but I couldn't find any. By my recollection of the creature the night before in relation to the trees and rocks in the immediate area, I estimated it must have been about 9 feet tall. I continued looking around on the ground, because I thought there must be tracks somewhere. The campsite next to us was vacant, but I remembered that there had been people there the day before, and they had packed up and left late in the afternoon, just before nightfall. I also remembered that a couple of them had sidearms, and I wondered if they had seen or heard something the night before, causing them to carry weapons. While I was considering this, Ralph walked over and said he wanted to pack up and go home. I tried to talk him into staying, but he was adamant. I asked him again what he thought it was that we had seen the night before, but his reply was that he didn't know, and he didn't want to talk about it. Our wives walked up, and they asked us if we had come to any conclusions as to what had happened. I told them no and informed them that Ralph wanted to pack up and go home. "What? What do you mean you want to go home? What happened Ralph?" Olivia asked. Ralph angrily shot back that he didn't want to talk about it. Olivia was shocked by his response, because it just wasn't like him to lose his cool like that. She tried to get him to talk, but he wasn't about to do so, because the only thing on his mind was packing up and getting the heck out of there. The kids were terribly disappointed, but we got everything together and headed back to Los Angeles.

While driving,I replayed the previous night's events over and over in my mind. What was that thing? Why wouldn't Ralph talk about what terrified him? Again and again, I tried to make some kind of sense of it all but simply couldn't come up with any kind of a reasonable explanation. I was also thinking about this being the first time I had gone camping since I was a Boy Scout, and all the great times I had, as a youngster, going to that camp on the Russian River in northern California. My home life wasn't very happy when I was a boy, so I really looked forward to getting away for two weeks every summer and spending time with friends. It was always an adventure that I didn't want to end.

For some reason, my name at camp was "Chief Stick In The Mud," but I was very proud of having won merit badges for archery, canoeing, life-saving and swimming, and I was well on my way to becoming an Eagle Scout. I got into trouble one time for stealing some girl's clothes off the clothesline and hanging them from the flagpole. Even the memory of having to peel potatoes for a week as punishment was a happy one, which should give you some idea as to just how ecstatic I was to be away from all the problems at home. But, this particular camping trip I had just experienced at Lake Isabella, was far removed from those happy days when I was a young Boy Scout. This was going to be the first vacation that we, as a family, had been on in years, and look what happened. It sure wasn't like camping as I remember it. Then I was pulled out of my thoughts when I realized my wife was calling my name. "Why are you so quiet?" she asked. "It's certainly not like you." My response was "Oh nothing. I'm just trying to figure out what happened last night. By the way, Bette, what exactly do you remember?" "Well, it was Puffy's barking that awakened me. He didn't sound as though he was afraid, but more like he was issuing a warning to whatever it was to stay away." Urging her to continue, I asked her if she heard anything else, and she said they heard something hit the side of the trailer. Nobody had mentioned this before. "Like what? What did it sound like?" I asked. "We just heard a thud," Bette replied. "Yeah dad, we thought you were trying to scare us!" chimed in the kids, and I assured them that whatever they heard was not caused by me. Hoping to jog their memory, I asked them if they were sure that all they heard was a thud and nothing else. They all admitted hearing Ralph's screams, and then my rushing through the trailer door. My wife said she had never seen me so frightened in the nine years we'd been married, and that I was pale as a ghost. "John, you can tell me, what was it that frightened you so?" "I honestly can't explain it. There was nothing horrendous about it, and it didn't make any advances toward us. It was really strange, almost like it could read my mind, and, although I couldn't see any eyes, I felt as though it was looking at me. This morning, when I asked Ralph what he saw, he said that it was a bear or a deer, and that he didn't want to talk about it. I know that it was definitely not a bear or deer or any other animal." We rode along in silence for a while, and then I remembered overhearing Ralph tell Olivia that it was like he had seen himself through eternity. What did that mean?

I realized Ralph was speeding down the highway. He wasn't interested in letting me lead the way when we left the campground and hadn't even bothered to stop and check out with the park ranger. It was as if he wanted to put as much distance as he could between us and the campground as quickly as

6

possible. I was hoping that he would slow it down here in the mountains, because there were some very sharp turns. We finally reached the summit and started our descent, and I noticed then that it was a CAVU day, which is pilot talk for clean air visibility unlimited. You could see for a hundred miles across the desert from that vantage point. I had seen the desert a on several occasions when I was flying a small plane. In fact, one of my first solo cross- country flights was to the Mojave Airport, and, since that first flight, I've had occasion to fly over the Mojave a few more times.

"Look everyone, there's Edwards Air Force Base." I said, as I pointed to the control tower. "Hey, dad, what kind of plane is that?" Jacob asked, pointing just north of Edwards. I tried to make out what type of aircraft it was, but for the life of me, I could not, because it appeared to be triangular in shape. Suddenly it made a 90 degree turn and then shot straight up. "Wow, that's one heck of an aircraft to be able to make a right angle turn at that speed and then ascend straight up. It must be some new aircraft the military is test-ing," I said. I explained to the kids that the Air Force regularly tested out new equipment at Edwards.

Ralph had the pedal to the metal now that we had reached the desert, and the trailer was swaying back and forth. I remember wishing that he would slow down, because it looked like he might lose it. I started to blink my lights, with the hope that he would realize how fast he was driving, but to no avail. "Oh, my God," my wife screamed. The trailer broke loose from the hitch and was going across the highway on it's own. I could see Ralph's brake lights, as the trailer crossed right in front of an oncoming car and headed into the desert. Fortunately, the driver of the car was able to avoid disaster. I could see the looks on the kids' faces in the rear view mirror. Their eyes were as wide as saucers, and Puffy was barking wildly, apparently sensing the panic we were all feeling. All you could see was a cloud of dust where the trailer had gone off the road. I braked and pulled over to the shoulder, and I noticed that Ralph was backing up. I glanced across the road toward the trailer and saw that it had finally come to a stop, and, thankfully, it remained upright. "Ralph, what happened?" I asked. As he stood there scratching his head, he said "I don't know. I just saw sparks, and then I saw the trailer zig zagging across the high-way behind me. It scared all of us." As we walked over to the trailer, I looked up and saw the same aircraft that we had spotted earlier. "Ralph, look at that." I said. "What is it, John?" he asked. "I don't know. It must be some new type of aircraft." "Did you notice that it doesn't make any sound?" he asked. Before I could respond, the craft shot off again. "Wow, that thing can move awfully fast. I've never seen anything like it."   We walked over to the trailer to inspect the damage. The first thing we looked at was the hitch, because we assumed that it must have broken. Strangely, other than being scratched up, it looked fine. We checked out the hitch on Ralph's car, and it, too, was undamaged. "Ralph, are you sure you hooked it up right?"   "I thought so, but maybe I didn't. I don't know John. Maybe because of all that happened ....well, maybe I didn't." "Ralph, do you want to talk about what happened last night?" "No!" Ralph angrily shot back. "Okay, okay. Maybe later." Ralph gave me a nod, and with that, we hooked the trailer back up and headed home.

Chapter 3
Back Home

Once we were home and settled, I decided that I needed to try to talk to Ralph and see if I could get more information from him. Olivia came to the door when I knocked. She invited me in, but told me Ralph was out, so I took the opportunity to question her as to whether or not Ralph had said anything else about what had happened. She said he told her that the "thing" we saw was not human. I asked her if she had heard anything hit the trailer, and she told me she had and that it was a frying pan. "A frying pan? What do you mean?" Apparently, Ralph saw the "thing" standing next to me and threw the first thing he could grab, which was the frying pan. It went right through the "thing" and hit the trailer. I decided that must have been what Bette and the kids had heard. "You mean he saw it standing next to me?" I asked. "Yes" she replied. I asked if Ralph mentioned what it was doing. She said he wouldn't say anything more, and he broke down and started to cry. I asked her what he was crying about, and her reply was that she wasn't sure, but she knew that whatever he saw put the fear of God into him.

Chapter 4
The Ouija Board

A few nights later, Carla, who was another of our neighbors, came over to the house. "What's under your arm, Carla?" I asked. " A Ouija Board." I didn't know what she was talking about, because I had never heard of a Ouija Board. I poured her a soda while we were waiting for my wife to join us, and she began setting up the Ouija Board on the kitchen table. I asked her to show me how it worked, and she told me to put my fingers on the pointer and ask the board a question. I thought it was rather ludicrous, but I decided to play along with her. I asked the board where I was going to be traveling to the following week. I sat there and waited for the pointer to move, but nothing happened. My wife walked into the room and was curious as to what we were doing, so I explained that I was trying to get the board to respond to me, but that so far nothing had happened. Then Carla tried, and she asked the same question -- "Where is John going next week." All of a sudden, to my astonishment, the pointer started to move to the letters H-A-W-A-I-I. I was skeptical and asked her if she knew about my upcoming trip, but she denied having any knowledge of my plans. My wife was excited, and she wanted to try her hand at it. She asked it the names of our children, and the pointer moved and spelled out the names of both our son and our daughter perfectly. She thought it was pretty amazing, but I still remained a skeptic. I told her to ask it something that she didn't know the answer to, and she asked the board to tell her where Carla was born. The pointer moved to the letters J-O-P-L-I-N. I asked Carla if that was where she was born, and she responded yes, that she had been born in Joplin, Missouri. I found that to be somewhat of a coincidence, because I was born in Independence, Missouri. My wife and I decided to ask it questions together, but after about a half hour or so, I felt exhausted and decided to take a short nap. I relaxed on the sofa while they continued with the Ouija Board. I guess I had fallen asleep, because I awoke with a start, sitting up suddenly, and found the women staring at me. I asked them what was wrong, and they told me they had asked the board if there was someone here, and it spelled out J-O-H-N H-O-L-M-E-S. John Holmes was my name at birth, but when my mother was divorced and remarried, my name was changed to John Clark. My wife was concerned that the board must be referring to my real father, and that maybe he had died and his spirit was in the room, but when they asked the board if it was referring to my father, it said no. My wife felt that somehow they had contacted my spirit, and she started to ask it some very personal questions. She said she thought they had someone or something else on the board. My curiosity got the better of me, so I got up from the couch to see what was going on. I asked her what she had meant by that statement, and she said it kept spelling out Q-O-N C-A-L-L-I-N-G, Q-O-N C-A-L-L-I-N-G. When we asked what Q-O-N was, it spelled out C-E-N-T-R-A-L C-O-M-M-U-N-I-C-A-T-I-O-N-S F-O-R E-V-E-R-Y P-L-A-N-E-T I-N T-H-E U-N-I-V-E-R-S-E. When they asked what his name was, he replied P-O-Z-A-N. At this point, the ladies and the Ouija Board definitely had my interest. I asked them if they thought they could try and get in touch with him again. They said they weren't sure, but that they would give it a try. I told them to ask the board what I had come in contact with while in Sequoia, and it responded K-N-O-W-N A-S B-I-G-F-O-O-T. A-L-I-E-N C-R-A-S-H-E-D 1-8-6-3 F-R-O-M P-L-U-T-O. I had them ask what this supposed alien was doing in our camp, and the board answered T-R-Y-I-N-G T-O W-A-K-E J-O-H-N. They asked the board why. Y-O-U C-A-N H-E-L-P was the reply. They asked why its own people couldn't help, and the response was N-O L-O-N-G-E-R L-I-F-E O-N P-L-U-T-O. I started to feel like I must be going crazy talking to this absurd board. I decided to ask it a question that nobody in the room could possibly know the answer to, including me. I asked what my boss Herb was doing, and the board answered that H-E I-S I-N H-A-W-A-I-I. What's he doing in Hawaii, we asked? S-A-I-L-I-N-G was the response. Well, I knew that couldn't possibly be true, because I knew that Herb didn't like sailing. I had tried to get him to go with me a few years before, and he told me that he would never go sailing if he could help it. I decided to check it out and see just what Herb was up to in order to clear this whole thing up right away. I dialed Herb's number, and the maid answered, informing me that Herb and his wife were out. I asked when they would return, and she told me they'd be back the next day. I then asked her where they went, and when her reply was Hawaii, the hair stood up on the back of my neck. I got the phone number where they could be reached and called right away. I asked for Mr. Marsh's room, and the hotel operator informed me that Herb wasn't in his room. I asked if he had left a number where he could be reached, and he informed me that it would be a little difficult to reach Mr. Marsh at the moment, because he was sailing. I was speechless. The operator thought the line had gone dead, until I finally regained my composure and thanked him before hanging up. I turned around to my wife and Carla and told them I couldn't believe it, but the board was right. Herb really is in Hawaii and has gone sailing. My wife thought I was kidding, but I assured her I was not. I decided to ask the board some more questions. "Okay Pozan, let's say that you really are from another planet. Where is your planet in relation to the planet earth?" The answer to this question was I-N G-A-L-A-X-Y B-E-Y-O-N-D Y-O-U-R-S. Next, we asked him if he knew the reason for planet earth, and the letters E-X-P-E-R-I-M-E-N-T were spelled out. "What kind of experiment," I asked. T-O S-E-E I-F Y-O-U C-A-N L-I-V-E I-N P-E-A-C-E T-O-G-E-T-H-E-R was the response, so I asked why, and I received the answer S-O W-E C-A-N A-L-L B-E T-O-G-E-T-H-E-R T-O L-I-V-E. I asked what we needed to learn in order to live in peace together, and the response was L-O-V-E T-H-E O-N-E-S Y-O-U L-O-V-E A-N-D L-E-A-R-N T-O G-I-V-E. I asked how we were doing, and the reply was M-U-C-H T-O-O S-L-O-W, Y-O-U W-I-L-L F-I-N-D-O-U-T T-H-E T-R-U-T-H A-B-O-U-T Y-O-U-R-S-E-L-V-E-S B-Y T-H-E Y-E-A-R 2-0-0-4. Next, I asked about Jesus Christ and whether he had been here on earth. Y-E-S was the response. I asked where he came from, and the answer was H-E I-S O-N-E O-F U-S. I wondered what the meaning of that was. The pointer went on to spell out the words N-O-T F-R-O-M T-H-E P-L-A-N-E-T E-A-R-T-H, T-H-E-R-E A-R-E M-A-N-Y A-L-I-E-N-S T-H-A-T A-P-P-E-A-R A-S H-U-M-A-N. I asked why that is so, and the board responded T-O E-N-H-A-N-C-E H-U-M-A-N I-N-T-E-L-L-I- G-E-N-C-E. I asked whether I already knew any of these aliens that are posing as humans. Y-E-S came the answer, J-A-C-K R-O-B-I-S-C-H-O-N. Jack was someone we had known when we lived in Hollywood. I always felt that Jack was a little far out, but never thought that he was an alien. I had lost contact with Jack some years before, so I asked if there were anyone else, and it answered Y-E-S, M-I-K-E P-A-T-R-I-C-K. I was still in contact with Mike, so I got on the phone right away. After I explained to Mike what I was calling about and what the board had said, he told me that he knew what I was talking about. I couldn't help but think to myself that it seemed as though everyone had gone off the deep end. Mike told me he needed to go to the site where I had my encounter, because he had experienced something very strange in the Rocky Mountains. He had back-packed into the mountain range and come upon a cabin. He entered the cabin and found everything inside to be in shambles. There was a mattress that was almost ripped in half leaning up against a potbellied stove, and it looked as though it had blood stains on it. It appeared as if someone was trying to protect himself from something. I asked him to hold on for a moment and had Carla ask the board what Mike had encountered. D-E-M-O-N, E-V-I-L, B-A-D came the reply. I got chills when I saw that answer. I told Mike what the board had said and that I felt he shouldn't even consider going back to Sequoia. I told him I'd give him a a call in a few days. I then asked Pozan if I knew any other "aliens." When I saw the answer was Y-E-S, Y-O-U J-O-H-N, I thought oh boy, this is going a little too far for me. P-R-E-V-I-O-U-S L-I-F-E R-U-L-E-R O-F M-A-R-S, H-A-D W-A-R W-I-T-H R-A-H, S-T-O-L-E R-A-H-S D-A-U-G-H-T-E-R, R-U-T-H-L-E-S-S R-U-L-E-R E-X-P-E-L-L-E-D F-R-O-M M-A-R-S, S-E-N-T T-O E-A-R-T-H T-O L-E-A-R-N H-U-M-I-L-I-T-Y. Well, if I did all of that to Rah, he must be pretty upset. N-O, S-A-D came the answer. I decided to try a different subject for awhile. I asked who killed Robert Kennedy. I-L-L-U-M-I-N-A-T-I was the reply, and my next question was "What is Illuminati?" A-L-I-E-N-S T-R-Y-I-N-G T-O D-E-S-T-R-O-Y T-H-I-S E-X-P-E-R-I-M-E-N-T. I told my wife that this was the second time I had heard the name Illuminati, the other time being when I heard someone on a radio talk show say that the name Illuminati was found in Sirhan's notebook, and that the notebook had disappeared.

We asked the board questions every day for about three weeks. One night when we were working the board, Puffy's hackles suddenly went up, and he started to growl ferociously. I checked outside to see if anyone was around and saw nothing. My wife asked the board what happened, and the reply came back that A D-E-M-O-N H-A-D T-R-I-E-D T-O C-O-M-E T-H-R-O-U-G-H, and when she asked the board if it could keep the demon out, it replied Y-E-S. At that point, I said, "Look Pozan, I really don't believe you are an alien, and if you are, I'll go out and look up in the sky, and you should be able to give me some type of signal." His reply was I C-A-N-T D-O T-H-A-T. "Why not", I asked, and it replied I A-M I-N A-N-0-T-H-E-R G-A-L-A-X-Y. I was exasperated, so I asked "Can't you do something to prove it to me?" I W-I-L-L W-O-R-K O-N I-T was the rather vague answer. I looked at my wife and told her to get rid of the board and told her that I had been doing some research on the Ouija Board, and nearly every source says that it's evil. She called Carla right away and asked her to come over to pick up her board. When Carla arrived, I asked her how long she'd had the board, and she told me about a month. I asked if anything strange or unusual had happened during that time, and she said, now that I mentioned it, she had been having some very strange nightmares. I asked her to describe them to me, and she said she would wake up in the night feeling as though she had been raped, but that she didn't feel her dreams had anything to do with the Ouija Board. I told her that I thought that maybe it did have something to do with her nightmares, and I advised her to get rid of it right away. Carla thought about it for a minute, and she asked me again if I really thought it was the cause of her dreams. I told her I wasn't positive, but I thought there was a significant chance that it might, somehow, be the reason. Finally, she agreed to let me get rid of the board, and I immediately took it outside and threw it in the dumpster, with the hope that would be the end of that.

Chapter 5
Oak Island

A few weeks later, while going over everything in my mind, I remembered reading an article about Oak Island in Nova Scotia. This was a small island near Halifax that I had visited in 1974, and I found it to be a very interesting place. My mind went back to the first night with the Ouija Board, and it had mentioned Oak Island, too. I didn't think much about it at the time, but it was in my notes as to what it had brought up that first night. TREASURE? Legend has it that approximately 150 years ago, two boys found a depression in the ground. Directly above the depression, there was a tree branch with marks on it indicating that someone had used a block and tackle to lower something into the ground. A group of explorers began to dig. At the ten-foot mark they discovered a platform of charcoal, coconut mats and oak. They removed that platform and continued to dig, and after going down another ten feet, they found another platform. Over several years, various people continued to dig, and every ten feet, they found one of the platforms. When they finally reached 198 feet, they found a clay seal which, according to the story, they felt was a warning. There was a stone tablet with hieroglyphics on it affixed to the clay. Rumor has it that someone from Ohio stole the tablet before anyone was able to decipher the hieroglyphics. Once they broke through the clay seal, water rushed into the tunnel. It was discovered that there were five tunnels leading to the ocean that would flood the chamber. It reminded me of the pyramids in Egypt. Over the years many people looked for the treasure, and one man, by the name of Blakenship, dug a parallel pit and then dug a tunnel alongside the "money pit" (the area where the treasure was supposedly buried). Mr. Blakenship then put a camera into the money pit, and the photograph showed a hand on top of a treasure chest. I saw the pictures, but they were very blurry, so you just had to take the word of Mr. Blakenship. As I was leaving the island, I noticed some people who appeared to be looking for the treasure, so I asked them if they had found anything. They showed me what they believed to be an old pier that someone had used to dry dock their ships to repair them. They also showed me pieces of wood that had old Spanish nails in them. As I was walking toward my car, I noticed a piece of wood to one side with one of those nails in it. I picked it up and took it with me.

I remembered that my wife had asked the Ouija Board whether there was buried treasure on Oak Island. Y-E-S. She then asked who put it there. S-P-A-N-I-S-H was the reply. If this were true, it could be the Inca treasure that the Spanish had stolen. When asked where the treasure was located, it replied B-Y T-H-E P-I-E-R I-N T-H-E S-A-N-D. I asked if it was the same pier that had been uncovered while I was there. Y-E-S. I should be able to easily find it then. N-O, T-O-O W-E-L-L H-I-D-D-E-N was the reply. T-H-E-R-E A-R-E C-O-N-D-I-T-I-O-N-S. I asked what they were. D-A-M-N Y-O-U-R S-O-U-L was the reply. "Well, forget it then" I said, "because no treasure is worth your soul." "Would anyone ever find it I asked?" Y-E-S, S-O-M-E-D-A-Y, I-F T-H-E-Y A-R-E W-I-L-L-I-N-G T-O P-A-Y T-H-E P-R-I-C-E.

Chapter 6
Superstition Mountain

When I was traveling through Arizona on a business trip, I decided to pay a visit to Superstition Mountain. I had read about the Lost Dutchman's Mine and had always wanted to go check it out, but I found myself a bit apprehensive, because, according to legend, many people had disappeared looking for this mine. There were several theories, such as they were abducted by UFOs, that other prospectors killed them to protect their claim or that they were killed by Indians. As I crested the hill, I saw Weaver's Needle, and it looked just as it had been described in the book, but something about it felt very eerie to me. As I was walking in, I came across some backpackers coming out, and I noticed that they were all wearing sidearms. I asked them what it was like in there, and one of them replied that it was weird. I then recalled one of the stories in the book about a team that had gone into the mountains. I think there were six of them, and they had a radio pack in order to stay in constant communication with someone on the outside. The second day, they lost communication with the team, so a search party was sent in to look for them. All of the equipment was found but no people, no bodies, nothing. Suddenly, I was startled by someone behind me. "I know why you're here." I turned around and found myself face to face with an old Indian man. My heart nearly leapt out of my chest! He introduced himself as the chief of the local Apache tribe. I asked how he knew why I was there, and he told me that he had a vision. "A vision of what?" I asked skeptically. "I had a vision that you would be here. Spirits in the sky told of your coming." I was beginning to think this must be part of a gimmick the park used for visitors, but I continued to listen to him. I asked him if he could tell me why so many people had disappeared. "Disturbed great spirits in the sky." I asked him if the Lost Dutchman's Gold Mine really existed. "Did not belong to white man." I asked him again if it really existed, and his answer was "Yes". I asked him if he knew where it was. "Yes." I asked him if he could take me to the treasure. "You are not ready," so I asked him when I would be ready. "You will know." I decided I'd had enough of Superstition Mountain. I said goodbye to the chief and walked away. "We will meet again." I picked up my pace a bit then. Boy, I sure can attract them, I thought to myself. I was happy to get to my car and put some miles between me and Superstition Mountain.

Chapter 7
Hawaii

Ladies and gentlemen, if you look out the right side of the aircraft, you can see the Big Island of Hawaii. There it is, I thought to myself, and it sure looks magnificent! It was another one of my business trips, and my first trip to Hawaii, so I was really excited. Then I saw Diamond Head, and it looked fabulous, just as depicted in all the pictures I had seen. When we landed, I took a deep breath, inhaling the delightful fragrance of gardenias. What a paradise! I picked up my rental car and headed for my hotel near the airport. Once I was settled in, I asked for directions to Waikiki Beach, because I couldn't wait to go for a swim. When I got there, I rushed right to the beach, threw my towel on the sand and ran for the water. It was wonderful, everything I thought it would be and more. After a few hours at the beach, I gathered up my belongings and headed back to the hotel. I was pretty tired, so I decided to order room service and relax in front of the television. Suddenly I had this strange feeling that there was someone else in the room. I got up and looked in the bathroom and in the closet, but found nothing. There was a knock at the door, which gave me quite a start, but it was just room service delivering my dinner. After I began eating, once again I felt the strange presence in the room. I looked around for the second time and still didn't find anything. I came to the conclusion that I must really be tired and imagining things, so I stretched out on the bed. I don't know how long I was asleep, but I awoke with a start and felt that same presence, but much stronger this time. It really spooked me, so I decided to leave the room and go out to the lobby. I sat down on one of their couches, and the next thing I knew, someone was trying to wake me to see if I was okay. I told them I was fine, and I headed back to my room. When my head hit the pillow, I was gone once again. I awakened to the first rays of sunlight coming through my window. After getting up and having a cup of coffee, I decided I would spend the day exploring the island, my first stop being Pearl Harbor. I took the boat out to the Arizona Memorial, and I found it to be a very sobering experience to look at the long list of names on that huge plaque and realize how many lives were actually lost in Pearl Harbor that fateful day. It was much more of an emotional experience than I had thought it would be, and several other people that were there had the same reaction. I took the boat back to shore and asked around for the best place to go for seafood, and I was referred to a place in Pearl City, so that's where I headed next.

After eating, I started to get that feeling again that I wasn't alone. After leaving the restaurant, I saw a church and decided to stop in, as I felt I really needed to talk to someone about what was going on with me. I noticed that there were three or four people sitting in a room inside the church, and I asked if I could talk to a priest. Everyone departed, except for a priest, who was sitting behind a desk. I guess I must have looked a little upset, because he immediately got up and escorted me down the hall to his office. I then proceeded to tell him my story, beginning with the camping trip in Sequoia, then about the Ouija Board and ending with my experiences since arriving on the island. He told me that what I encountered was Satan. I thought I must have misunderstood him, so I asked him again, and, once again, he said I encountered Satan. He said that Satan sometimes presents himself in a physical form when he feels that someone is a threat or will become a threat to him. I asked him about the Ouija Board saying to love the ones you love and learn to give. His reply was that Satan will tell you whatever you want to hear, up to and including the scriptures. We talked for about an hour, and I felt a lot more at ease having shared my concerns with someone. I wasn't feeling too good about the priest thinking that I was dealing with Satan, however. I thanked him for taking the time to listen to me, and he told me to come back whenever I felt the need.

When I returned to my car and unlocked the door, much to my chagrin, I found a large rock on the driver's seat. I asked one of the locals if it had some meaning, and he told me that I would soon sleep with the fish. The blood drained from my face, I'm sure. I asked him why someone would give me such a message, and he explained that I must have broken a taboo and offended Madam Pele. He said Madam Pele was the Hawaiian Volcano Goddess. I told him that I couldn't imagine how I had offended her, and he said that the removal of any rocks from the islands was strictly forbidden. I remembered that I had picked up a rock the day before when I was out sightseeing. I asked the man what I could do to get back in Madam Pele's good graces, and he advised me to put the rock back where I found it. Since I wasn't entirely certain exactly where I had picked up the rock, I wasn't able to put it back right where I had found it, but I did leave the rock in Hawaii. The rest of my stay there was uneventful, and I certainly was thankful for that!!

Chapter 8
Twisters

    Welcome to Omaha, the flight attendant announced. Omaha was my next assignment, and it was only the second time I had been there, the other time being in 1972. It was extremely humid, I noticed, when I stepped out of the airport door. When I arrived at my hotel, I asked the young lady behind the desk if they got many tornados, and she smiled and said not to worry, because even though Omaha is in what is called "tornado alley", they really didn't get many of them. After getting settled in my room, I decided to go over to Aksarben (Nebraska spelled backwards) Race Track to try my luck. I remembered from my previous visit that it was a beautiful track. After the second race, the announcer told us to take immediate cover due to high winds. As I started to file down the stairs to the shelter, I asked the person next to me what this meant, and he said it was probably a tornado. I noticed that everyone seemed to be taking it in stride, so I didn't feel that I should be alarmed, so I took my time walking down the ramp, as I followed everyone into the shelter area.   Suddenly, it got really quiet, and then it sounded like a freight train was going by, which was the description I'd always heard of an approaching tornado. We were down in the shelter for about twenty minutes before they gave us the all clear to go back up top. When I got back up, I couldn't believe my eyes. All the houses on the hill about a block from the track were leveled. It looked like the tornado's path may have gone in the direction of my hotel, so I headed to the parking lot. I was starting out the gate, when a security guard asked me where I was going. I told him I was going back to my hotel, but he advised against it, saying that another tornado could very possibly be on the way. I told him I'd take my chances. I couldn't believe the destruction I encountered on the way back to the hotel. Cars were thrown up on the hillside and steel girders were twisted. I had no idea the wind was capable of doing this much damage. As I pulled up to my hotel, I was horrified by what I saw. The majority of the hotel was in shambles, so I immediately parked the car and got out to inspect more closely. The young lady that had checked me in was out in front, and she was in tears. She looked at me and asked how I knew that a tornado was going to hit, so I assured her that I hadn't had any idea that this was going to happen. I walked over to what had once been my room to see if anything was left, but everything was gone. I phoned my boss, Herb, in Los Angeles, to give him the news. I told him he wouldn't believe what had just happened, but before I could finish, he said "Yes, he had just seen footage of the destruction on the news." I told him that I would be on the first flight out and would see him soon. I checked with the hotel manager about insurance and was on my way out of Nebraska, thankful that I was still alive.

Chapter 9
Tornado

A few months after my Omaha trip, I was in Cleveland, Ohio, on yet another business trip. I was watching a game on the television in the lounge of the hotel, when a banner flashed across the bottom of the screen announcing that a tornado warning was in effect. My first thought was that this couldn't possibly be happening to me again. I told the man sitting next to me that he would be well advised to move to another chair, because something may be after me, which elicited a rather condescending look that I was very familiar with by now.   Fortunately, a short time later, they gave an all clear. I then contacted a friend of mine in Cleveland, and he invited me to go out to the lake with him and his kids to do a little fishing. I said I'd love to, but I didn't have my fishing pole with me, but he said not to worry, because he had extras. I asked him if he was worried about the weather being a little unsettled, but he assured me it was a good time to go fishing. He told me not to be concerned, because they have tornado watches all the time, and they never materialize. When we got to the lake, we went down to the boat dock, and as we were putting all of our gear in the boat, I asked Tony what kind of fish we were going after. He said we would be fishing for bass, which sounded great to me, as bass were my favorite fish to catch. Once we were all situated in the boat, we cast off. Tony caught the first fish, which was a really nice big mouth bass. It must have weighed in at a minimum of four pounds. "The next one is mine," I announced, but both of his kids were determined to prove me wrong. It wasn't long until little Tony was pulling in a crappie, and his brother had a small mouth bass on his hook. We were nearing the beach, and since everyone had to go to the bathroom, we docked the boat. We all got a soda and a hot dog from the food stand, since all that rigorous fishing had made us very hungry and thirsty, and then, once again, we all piled into the boat and headed back. Just as we rounded a bend, there was a big, black cloud coming in low, heading right for us. The clouds that were in the movie, Close Encounters, reminded me of this one. "Get the boat turned around quick!" shouted Tony, and the urgency in his voice made me believe that we were in for trouble. By the time we got back to the beach, the life guards were blowing their whistles and telling everyone to clear the area. We were told to take immediate cover, but we didn't need any encouragement to hustle. We had the boat docked and were running for shelter before you could whistle Dixie. We headed for the bathroom area, since it seemed to be the only place that could offer reasonable shelter, and just as I reached that point, I could see the trees beginning to bend in the wind. I was really getting nervous as I sat crouched against the wall, and couldn't help but think about the Wizard of Oz, and whether I would have the same fate as Dorothy. "Oh, please God, don't let this happen," I prayed, while at the same time, I tried to appear confident for the sake of the children. The wind was really beginning to get strong, and I could see the fear on everyone else's face, knowing that I probably had that same look on mine. I just hoped that the cinder wall that we were behind was going to hold, and, thank God, it did. It seemed like an eternity before it was over. My mind kept returning to Sequoia, the Ouija Board, Hawaii and Omaha. I was wondering what was happening to me, when I was brought back to reality by the lifeguards' whistles blowing the all clear. I breathed a sigh of relief that we had been spared. The tornado had just missed us, I later found out. I couldn't wait to get back to my room.

After the day at the lake, I decided it was time to talk to someone again about what was going on with me. I went to a Franciscan monastery and talked to a monk. After telling him everything, he told me to sit still and listen while he prayed for me. He was very nice, but I couldn't help but think that perhaps he thought I was a little off my rocker; but then, who could blame him?

Chapter 10
The Exorcism

I began desperately trying to find someone who could give me answers, or at least peace of mind, as to what was happening in my life. I tried the Episcopal Church, the Roman Catholic Church and the Lutheran Church. I even ended up having an exorcism. I asked the priest if he was certain the exorcism would work, and he said absolutely. I prayed he was right, because I truly didn't know just how much more I could take. My entire life was being affected, including my marriage and my job.

Chapter 11
Stalled Engines

In 1979, I once again found myself back in Hawaii. Some friends of mine, who I grew up with, knew I had quit working for Herb and asked me to go to Hawaii with them to talk about a business proposition. They also wanted to cheer me up, since I had recently divorced my wife. After spending a few days on Kauai, we were on our way to Hilo, on the big Island of Hawaii, because Ken wanted to look at some property there. We landed at the airport in Honolulu, where we had to change planes to fly on to Hilo. I went up to the desk to find out what was holding us up, and I was told that we had been bumped from our flight. They couldn't offer me any explanation, but we were definitely bumped, and they didn't have another flight for us to take. Ken was very upset, because he had made arrangements to meet someone, and the meeting couldn't be rescheduled. He remembered that I was a pilot and asked me if I could rent a plane and fly us over. I told him that we would need a twin engine for that many passengers, and that I wasn't qualified for twins. He told me to call and reserve a plane. I told him it would be quite expensive, but he didn't care, so I reserved the plane and the pilot. By the time we reached the other side of the airport, I noticed that they were pre-flighting our aircraft. One of the members of the pre-flight crew asked me if we wanted the bar on board set up, and I told her to go ahead. The pilot showed up and introduced himself as Phil. I asked Phil if he minded if I sat in the right seat. I showed him my pilot's license and explained that I would like to get a little twin time, and he said "Sure, no problem." Once everyone got aboard, I made certain that all seat belts were fastened, because I had noticed that my friends hadn't had any trouble finding the bar. "November 347 Whiskey Sierra ready to go," Phil radioed to the control tower. "Whiskey Sierra 347 cleared for take off," came back the tower. Phil asked me if I wanted to take control. It took me by surprise, because I had never flown a plane of that size, but he assured me that he would be right there, I guess because he could see the apprehension on my face. As I pushed the throttles forward, I could feel the difference between this and a single engine, and my adrenaline was really pumping. In no time, we were airborne. "Climb to 8500 feet and maintain the heading that you are on," said Phil. "Roger on that," I replied. I looked in the rear of the plane to see how my friends were faring. It appeared as though they were certainly enjoying themselves, and they were already pouring their second drink. I was admiring the beautiful scenery down below, when I saw that we were coming up on Maui. "There's Haliakala," I announced to everyone. "House of the sun," added Phil. I couldn't believe how beautiful it looked. We had passed over Haliakala and were over the channel between Maui and the Big Island. I could see the Big Island and remarked on the fact that it's larger than all of the other islands combined. Suddenly, the yoke was yanked out of my hand, and I could see that the engine on my side was quitting. As I turned to ask Phil what was wrong, I could see that the other engine was quitting, too. I asked him what he thought was going on, and he said he didn't know, but to let him have the yoke. I turned to look at the altimeter, and I noticed that we were dropping fast. I turned to the back of the plane and told my friends to get their life jackets on, but they thought I was kidding and told me to knock it off. I assured them that this was no joke, and that we were going down, and with our sink rate, I didn't think we would be able to make it back to land, so that they had better put their life jackets on right now. Since Phil had his hands full trying to get the engines started, I asked him if he wanted me to declare Mayday. I knew we had to do something fast, because the altimeter was at 2500 feet. All of a sudden, shark fins came to mind, and that this was probably going to be the end of me. Just as I was depressing the mic button to declare a Mayday, I could feel a lift. I looked out on my side and saw that my engine had started back up. I then looked at the port side and noticed that engine had started also. I asked Phil if we were all right, and he responded that he thought so. I asked him if we shouldn't land on Maui instead, but he said no, we'd go on to Hilo. I agreed, because after all, he was the boss, I told myself. All I knew was that I could see the Maui airport, and I could not see the Hilo airport. When we landed in Hilo, I said a prayer of thanks that we survived. After that trip, I told my friends I was heading back to the mainland for an interview, because I had decided that I was going to get a job in San Francisco and give up traveling.

Chapter 12
The Psychic

      I moved to San Francisco, because I landed a job at the San Francisco Newspaper Agency, which made me very happy. After being there about a year, I decided to tell my boss about my experiences. After listening to me, he advised me to get in touch with a friend of his, by the name of Fred, who claimed to be a psychic. I did so, and he advised me that what I had encountered had to do with aliens. Oh great, I thought, first Satan, then demons and now aliens. Fred gave me a telephone number for one of the top experts in UFO research, Dr. Richard Haines, who was a scientist at NASA, so I decided I'd call Dr. Haines and see what he had to say. I introduced myself and told him Fred Sanders had referred me to him, and it was Fred's opinion that I had an alien encounter. He acknowledged knowing Fred and said he would like to hear what had happened to me, and he asked me if I minded if he taped our conversation, which I agreed to. After I was finished with the interview, Dr. Haines said that he would get back to me in a couple of days, and just a few days later, he phoned me and asked if I could meet him for lunch. I said sure, and we made arrangements to meet at Coyote Point. During lunch, he told me that he had gone over our taped conversation, and he felt that I had a subjective reality, and that I really did see something on my camping trip. I told him that I knew what I saw on my camping trip was real, not some type of hallucination, but what I needed to know was what it was and why were these strange things happening to me. He told me that he didn't know what I encountered, but he felt that the strange events were just coincidences. I told him I didn't feel that they were coincidental, but I appreciated his taking the time to meet with me. I actually felt very encouraged, because he obviously believed that what I had told him did, in fact, occur as I described.

Chapter 13
Lake Tahoe

Approximately three weeks after my lunch with Dr. Haines, I was talking to my brother about Lake Tahoe. I told him that it had been about ten years since I'd been up there, and I'd really like to go back. So, he made the necessary arrangements to rent a condo for a few days, and he and his family went with me to Tahoe that weekend. We all traveled together in my brother's car, and when we reached the summit, I could see the lake in the distance, and it was even more beautiful than I remembered. I couldn't wait to test lady luck at the casinos, so once we were settled in at the condo, I asked if anyone felt like gambling. Everyone was tired, but my brother offered me his car, and off I went. I was surprised at the growth of South Shore. It seemed as though everywhere you looked, there was now a hotel or a restaurant. The first casino I came to was Harrah's, so I decided to bite the bullet and try my luck. Once inside, I headed straight for the first black jack table I saw. It immediately seemed as though this might be my lucky day! Before I knew it, I had won $500. After a couple of hours, I began to get a little tired, so I decided I better go back to the condo and get some rest before we went to the Glen Campbell show that night. I pocketed my winnings and was out the door. Back at the condo, everyone was sound asleep, and it wasn't long before I was, too. The next thing I knew, my sister-in-law was standing over me trying to wake me up to get ready to go to the show. I bounced right up, showered, shaved and dressed in no time at all, and we headed out the door on our way to the show room. While we were waiting to get into the show, I did a little more gambling on the slot machines and ended up winning a few more dollars. Eventually, we got into the packed show room, and it was a fantastic performance. During an intermission, on my way back from the men's room, I stopped at the black jack table and won a hundred dollars in just a few minutes. I was having a great time, and I'm sure I must have grinned as I thought to myself that I might be able to give up my day job if this keeps up! After the show, we played some more slot machines and black jack, and it looked as though my luck was still with me. My brother and his wife decided that they'd had enough and wanted to go back to the condo. I told them to go ahead, and I'd catch a cab when I was ready to leave. Eventually, however, my luck began to run out, so I thought I'd try another casino. I was crossing the street toward Harvey's, when I noticed that there was a Caesar's there. I had been to the one in Las Vegas, and I wanted to see how this one compared. As I was climbing the stairs inside the casino, I noticed that at the top there was an airplane hanging above a group of slot machines. I was so amazed, because I had seen casinos give away cars and boats before, but this was the first time I had seen an airplane as the prize. I stopped, put in three quarters and pulled the handle. I stared at the machine and thought it seemed rather strange that there were treble bars all on the bottom line. I thought I must have won something, but no quarters were dropping out, so I asked the change person behind me about it. He looked at my machine and told me I had just won the airplane. It didn't sink in. What airplane, I thought, and then I realized he meant the airplane above me. The news spread like wild fire through the casino, and the entertainers actually came off the stage to see who had just won the $42,000 airplane. I was in utter shock. I wondered if this is what Pozan had meant when he had said so very long ago that he would work on it. I just sat there on the stool, and then someone made the comment that I should be jumping up and down, because I had just won that airplane! I knew they wouldn't understand, so I didn't even try to explain. Someone was asking me for identification, and I came back to reality and handed them my pilot's license. They couldn't believe it. I was a pilot, and I had just won an airplane! What are the odds of a pilot winning an airplane, people were saying? Later, I realized it was a mistake to show them my pilot's license, because when I told them I'd rather have the cash than the plane, the casino informed me I had to take the plane. After all, they would get lots of publicity out of a pilot winning an airplane at their casino, and I was informed that I had to agree to appear on television to promote their casino.

Chapter 14
Hypnosis

When I returned to San Francisco, I called Dr. Haines, and he told me
that he had seen me on television. However, he still insisted that it was all a
coincidence. I went back to the psychic and told him what had happened. He
then got me in contact with Dr. James Harder, a professor at U.C.- Berkeley. I
telephoned Dr. Harder, and he asked me if I had ever been regressed. I told
him I didn't think that I had been, but I wasn't sure I understood exactly what
the term regression meant, and he explained that regression was hypnosis. I
told him that I had never been put under hypnosis, so he suggested that I come
to his home that afternoon. I agreed to accept his invitation, and after he gave
me the directions, I was on my way. When I arrived there, I was very
impressed. There was an elevator to take you up the hillside to his house, and it
reminded me of something one might see in a movie. As I stepped into the elevator, I became a little apprehensive, because it really didn't seem to be very
stable. My fears were unfounded however, because I made it to the top. The
view, as I got out of the elevator, was incredible, because you could see all the
way out to the Golden Gate Bridge. I knocked on the door, and a slight man,
wearing Bermuda shorts, greeted me. We introduced ourselves, and I compli-
mented him on his beautiful home. He offered me tea or coffee, and I accepted
a cup of coffee. Dr. Harder asked me to try to fill him in on everything that
had happened to me, beginning with Sequoia and ending with winning the airplane. After having done so, he asked me if I was ready to be regressed.
Having never been put under hypnosis, I was a little nervous, but I really wanted to find out if this would help me get the answers to all this craziness. I
reclined on Dr. Harder's couch, and I remember thinking it wasn't very com-
fortable. He told me to relax and start by taking some deep breaths. He continued talking to me about relaxing, and then he told me to go back to the night
of my camping trip in Sequoia. He asked me if I was back to that night, and I
said yes, but my speech seemed like it was in slow motion. I remember wondering if he might have put something in my coffee, which made me even
more apprehensive, but I told myself I had to go through with this.
Dr. HARDER: What do you see, John?
JOHN: Eyes.

DR. HARDER: What type of eyes?

JOHN: Very large.

DR. HARDER: What color are they?

JOHN: Yellow eyes with black slits.

DR. HARDER: What are you doing?

JOHN: I'm in a prone position. I don't feel anything under me, but I am in a prone position.

DR. HARDER: What is happening, John?

JOHN: They are putting tubes through my stomach and through my arms. How can this be? I don't feel any pain. They are very large tubes. I can't speak, but they are telling me not to be afraid---that it will be over in a short time. "What are they doing?" I thought to myself. Even though I didn't speak the question out loud, the response came back, "retrieval." I can't make out any mouths. Those eyes, they are really beginning to bother me. It's like looking through eternity. I feel like screaming, but I can't. Please God, help me. They are starting to do something else, but I cannot see.

I became very rigid and couldn't go any further with the hypnosis. Whatever they were doing, it was terrifying me. I guess Dr. Harder recognized that I was in great discomfort, so he began the process of waking me up, and I certainly was glad that he did. I asked him what he thought, and he told me that he was quite sure I had been abducted. He said he would like to regress me a couple more times before he could be certain whether or not I had, indeed, been abducted, and he asked if I wanted to set up another appointment. I told him I needed to think about it, and I would let him know. He told me to think it over, and he hoped he'd hear from me soon.

Driving home after my session, I kept wondering if this can really be happening to me? Am I in some kind of nightmare, and if I am, will someone please wake me up? "That will be a dollar, please", said the toll taker. How did I get to the Richmond/San Rafael Bridge already, I wondered? When I arrived at home, I called Fred and told him what had happened. He asked me what I thought, and I told him that I didn't know what to think anymore, because it's all happening too fast. "Besides," I told him, "you're the psychic, so why are you asking me?" He went on to remind me of what he had told me on my first visit to his office, which was that my experience had to do with aliens. I told him I remembered what he had said, but also that Dr. Haines had said it was all a coincidence. However, now Dr. Harder is telling me he thinks it's aliens. I didn't know who to believe or what to do next. I asked Fred if he thought I should go see Dr. Harder again, and he replied sure, why not, what can it hurt.

Chapter 15
Warren Hinkle

I was at Hanno's, a bar across the street from the San Francisco Chronicle and Examiner. "Mr. Hinkle, how are you doing?" I heard the bartender ask. Wow, Warren Hinkle, I thought to myself. Hinkle's a big shot writer for the Chronicle. I wonder if he could put me in touch with anyone who might be able to help me get some answers. I introduced myself to Mr. Hinkle and asked him if we could talk for a minute. He asked me if I was the guy who won the airplane in Tahoe, and I said yes. He asked me what he could do for me and I told him my whole story. Afterwards, I told him I knew that it was a little hard to swallow, but that it had all happened exactly the way I described. I told him about Dr. Harder wanting me to come back for more sessions, and that I was a bit apprehensive. I asked Warren if he had ever heard of Dr. Harder, and he said that he had, and that some people thought he was a little far out with his ideas about aliens and flying saucers. He suggested I make an appointment with Dr. Harder for the following Thursday, and he would go like to go along, if it was all right with me. I told him sure, I thought it would be great to have him sit in on a session. I also told him, however, that I would have to ask Dr. Harder if it would be all right to bring a guest. He gave me his card and asked me to call him as soon as I talked to Dr. Harder. I contacted Dr. Harder right away, and asked him about bringing Warren Hinkle with me to my next session, and he said it would be fine, so we set up an appointment for the following Thursday. I called Warren, and we made arrangements to meet beforehand at Hanno's and drive to Dr. Harder's together. When I arrived at Hanno's, Warren was there with his brother-in-law, Bill Johnson, and said he wanted to bring him along as an impartial witness. I told him that I didn't care, but that I hoped it would be okay with Dr. Harder. We arrived at Dr. Harder's office, and he said it was fine for Bill to sit in. We all got settled, and I was again put under hypnosis. After the session, Warren asked Dr. Harder what he had concluded, and he said he was 99% convinced that I had been abducted, not just once, but many times.

Warren wrote a full page article about my experiences and the session with Dr. Harder, but did I ever pay the price for that. All of my fellow workers at the newspaper started calling me ET, and a lot of them let me know that they thought I was crazy. As if I didn't already have enough to deal with, now this on top of it. I was just trying to live my life, and someone or something was interfering. One day, I walked into my office and someone had written on my desk "ET tastes like chicken." I know most people thought it was great fun to tease me and give me a hard time, but the harassment was difficult to deal with at times. Inside, I was crying out "I'm just like you! I am not a freak!"

Chapter 16
Tom Jolie

One day after work, I returned home to a message on my answering machine from someone named Tom Jolie. I returned his call, and he told me he was calling in regard to the newspaper article. He said he believed UFOs existed, and he wanted to talk to me about my experiences. I asked him who he worked for, and he told me Lockheed Missile Systems. I was a little leery, because I recalled Dr. Harder telling me to be careful who I talked to about this, as there were people who would try to kidnap and drug me to find out what I knew. I remembered telling Dr. Harder that they wouldn't have to drug me, because I'd gladly tell them anything they'd want to know. His response was "It's what you don't remember that they would want to find out." As I made arrangements to meet Tom at Zim's Restaurant the next day, Dr. Harder's warning was ringing in my ears. When I walked into

the restaurant, Tom walked over and introduced himself. He had something over his shoulder, and I asked him what it was. He said it was a video camera, and that he wanted to do a film on flying saucers. I thought to myself that I'd better beware of this guy, because something just didn't seem quite right to me. I relayed my story to him pretty much as it had appeared in Warren's newspaper article, and when I was done, Tom asked me if he could begin filming me on a continuing basis. I decided that in spite of my trepidation, I really didn't have anything to lose and agreed to let him do so.

Chapter 17
Psychic Institute

The next day, Fred telephoned me to let me know that he had set up a meeting for me at the Psychic Institute. He said he had told a group of the psychics at the institute my story, that they wanted to do a reading on me, and that the appointment was set for Saturday. The next morning, Tom Jolie called to see if I'd be available on Saturday to start filming. I told him about the Psychic Institute, and he asked if he could come along. I said sure, why not. I met Tom out in front of the institute, and he had, not only his camera, but a briefcase as well. I asked what was in the briefcase, and he told me he had brought along a few extra rolls of film and some papers. Inside the institute, there were about thirty or forty people milling about, and I asked if anyone had seen Fred. I was told that he was in the next room, and they would let him know I had arrived. He came out into the lobby and escorted us into the room. Before I knew it, I was sitting in front of all of these strangers, and they were telling me that they had never seen energy like mine, and that I frightened them. They also told me that I had the power to cure or kill them. Tom was sitting next to me looking rather skeptical, which was pretty much my reaction, as well. He said "Look, all of you people claim that you can see John's aura and all this other stuff. Well, I have a little test for you, which will tell me just how accurate you really are. I have a picture inside my briefcase that I'll show to John, and I would like to see if you can tell us what the picture is." One of the psychics objected and said they were not going to submit to carnival games. Tom responded that if they didn't agree to the test, he would advise me to leave this charade. I couldn't believe what I was hearing. I brought this guy with me as a guest, not as my keeper, but on the other hand, maybe he was just looking out for my best interests. One of the psychics asked me whether I was going to stay or go. I was feeling very uncomfortable and told them that perhaps it would be best if I would come back another time. I wanted nothing more than to get out of that place, so Tom and I left the institute and went to my house. When we arrived there, there was a message on my answering machine to call Diane at Channel Four. I asked Tom what he thought that was about, and when I turned around to look at him, he was filming me. I told him to please put the camera away and sit down, because I wanted to talk to him to find out what he thought about the psychics. He said he didn't believe anything they said, and that he thought they were nothing more than a bunch of charlatans. I asked him if he felt that way because they refused to submit to his test. He admitted that their refusal was part of the reason that he doubted their credibility. Just then, the phone rang, interrupting our conversation. It was Dr. Harder wanting to know if I had talked to Diane at Channel Four. I told him that I hadn't, and I asked him if he knew why she was calling. He said that the station wanted the two of us to appear on a talk show the following Tuesday, and that he had agreed to do so, with the hope that I would agree as well. I turned to Tom and told him what was going on and asked him what he thought about my appearing on the show. He suggested that I go ahead and do it, for the simple reason that it would help get my message out. I started to remember what happened to me when Warren Hinkle's story hit the paper, and all of the ridicule I suffered as a result. Tom told me not to worry, and that he'd help me get through it. I then told Dr. Harder that I would do the show.

Chapter 18
TV Show

The day of the show, Tom and I met Dr. Harder at Tommy's Joint, which was just down the street from the television station. I introduced Tom to Dr. Harder, and Tom told him that he had heard a lot about him. Dr. Harder questioned him as to exactly what it was he had heard. He said that Dr. Harder's name had come up many times in the UFO research he had done, especially in the research he did on Betty and Barney Hill and Travis Walton. Dr. Harder merely responded by saying "Yes, you do know what you're talking about," and then he turned away from Tom and looked at me. He asked me if I had ever done a television show, and I answered honestly by saying that I had not, and that I was somewhat apprehensive. He told me that there really wasn't anything to be nervous about, because he would be doing most of the talking, and since he had done many such shows,
he would be able to walk me right through it with no problem.   While we were waiting back stage, I noticed that they had set up a table of food for us. I went over and started to pick up something to eat, when I thought I noticed something in one of the bowls moving. I heard the announcer introduce the person appearing before us as someone who had written a book entitled Cooking With Insects. That's what was in the bowl, I realized, and I began to feel ill. When it was our turn to go on, my nervousness really began to kick in, and when the host of the show asked me a question, I froze. It was a good thing Dr. Harder was there to step in and help me out, and, needless to say, I was delighted that I wasn't asked any more questions. After the show, we ran into Fred back stage, and I assumed it must have been because Dr. Harder had told him we were going to be on television. Dr. Harder invited all of us to his house. I rode over with Tom. I felt it was very strange that he had no problem finding the house without having gotten any directions from me. We were all talking in Dr. Harder's living room, when Fred asked me to join him in the kitchen. Once we were out of earshot of the others, he asked me how I knew Tom. I explained that he telephoned me after he had seen Warren's newspaper article and the television news story about my winning the airplane. He asked me if I had wondered how Tom was able to get my phone number, since I had my number changed and unlisted, due to the fact I was receiving a lot of

harassing phone calls. That hadn't dawned on me until Fred mentioned it. He asked me where Tom worked, and when I told him Lockheed Missile Systems, he told me he was going to check him out. We went back to the living room and joined the others, and shortly thereafter, we wrapped up our meeting. As we were leaving, Fred pulled me aside and told me that Dr. Harder felt that I was one of them. "One of whom?" I asked. "Aliens", replied Fred. I asked him what he was talking about, and he told me he would call me later. Fred's remark was very upsetting to me, and I kept thinking about it on the ride back to Marin. Tom was trying to make small talk, but I wasn't paying much attention. He wanted to know what Fred talked to me about in the kitchen, and I told him we just talked about the show----nothing of any importance.

The next day, Fred called me and told me to get rid of Tom. When I asked him why, he told me he had done some research and found out that Tom was with military intelligence. I asked him how he had found that out, and he said that he had his sources. I was stunned and hung up the phone. I was to the point that I didn't know who or what to believe anymore. I felt paranoia settling in on me, and I tried to tell myself, once again, that this kind of thing happens only in the movies and in nightmares, and surely it will all end soon.

Chapter 19
Las Vegas

I decided I needed some time alone to think, so I got in my car and just started driving. I headed down the coast, and before I knew it, I was in Carmel. I stopped long enough to get something to eat and continued driving south, while I kept playing everything over and over in my head. I didn't stop the car until I reached Los Angeles, where I checked into a motel by the airport. I called my office and left word that I would be out for a few days. Next, I tried calling Rudy, who was a good friend I had met when I lived in Los Angeles. His number had been disconnected and directory assistance had no new listing for him. Suddenly, I was overwhelmed with the feeling that someone or something was in the room with me, just like had happened when I was in Hawaii, and my chest felt heavy from the fear I was experiencing. I told myself that if someone was after me, I was going to get them off the track, so I called the airport to see if they had a flight to Las Vegas. The last plane for the day departed in an hour. Without checking out of my motel in Los Angeles, I boarded the plane to Las Vegas, and, when I landed, I took a cab to Caesar's. I was amazed at how much Las Vegas had changed since the last time I was there in 1974. When I got to Caesar's, I went straight to the slot machines. I didn't win another airplane, but I did manage to win a $500 jackpot. After a few hours of gambling, I decided to get something to eat, and while I was eating, I kept going over everything, trying to make some kind of sense of it all. I decided to go back to Los Angeles in the morning, pick up my car and then head for home. Running away wasn't doing me any good. I checked into Caesar's for the night and couldn't help thinking how insane I was behaving by checking into two hotel rooms for the same night in two different cities. I realized that this was a good example of what fear can actually cause a person to do. The next morning, when I arrived back in Los Angeles, I phoned Fred and told him what I had done. I guess he was getting used to my occasional rash decisions, because he simply said that he had tried calling me many times and was getting quite concerned, thinking that maybe they had gotten to me again. I told him I would call him when I got home.

Chapter 20
UFOs

Arriving back in Marin, I picked up the newspapers that had piled up in front of my door and saw something on the front page of the local paper that caught my eye. The headline read "Marin Couple's Close Encounter." The article was about some people that lived about a mile from me who had spotted a flying saucer on two different occasions. My spirits soared with the hope that I might finally be able to talk with people who would understand what I'd been going through. I called the reporter who had done the story and asked him for the phone number of the couple. A woman answered the phone, and I introduced myself, explaining that I was calling about the article in the paper. She said she really regretted that her husband gave the interview, because they had received many screwball phone calls, but I assured her that I was serious, and that I knew what she was talking about. I asked her if she could describe the UFO to me, and she said it was triangular in shape, which struck me as being very odd. I asked her for the date of the first sighting, and after pausing for a moment, she finally said that it was February 19 at 2:30 a.m. I had to end the conversation at that moment, because I was overwhelmed. February 19 at 2:30 a.m. was the exact date and time that I had won the airplane. Just then, the telephone rang, and it was Warren Hinkle. He wanted me to meet him at his office, so we made plans to meet the next day after work.

When I walked into Warren's office the next afternoon, he asked me how I was doing. "Not too good," I replied. I asked him why he needed to see me, and he said he had received a phone call from a friend of his who worked at Caesar's Tahoe. She told Warren that she was on her way to work the night I won the airplane, and she saw something hovering over the Casino. She read Warren's article about me and called him right away. He asked her to describe what she saw, and she said that it was triangular in shape. She told Warren that many people had seen it, and it even made the front page of the local paper. Warren showed me the copy of the article, and I was beginning to feel as though I were sinking deeper and deeper into an abyss. I read the article, which was entitled "UFO's Over Tahoe." It described how the police had chased it, and that it was seen hovering over Caesar's Tahoe. I then told

Warren about the couple in Marin who had, on two separate occasions, seen an object fitting the same description. He told me that he had gone over the recording of my session with Dr. Harder, and I had described being in a triangular shaped room. I told him that was impossible, because I never thought of UFO's as being triangular in shape. I had always thought of them as being disc shaped, which is why I thought they were called flying saucers. However, I didn't realize that Warren had taped my session. He put the tape in a cassette player and told me to listen for myself. I was totally shocked when I actually heard myself describing a triangular room. Hearing my own words caused such stress, that I actually found myself having difficulty breathing. I asked Warren what he thought all of this meant. He said he didn't know, but he had called a friend of his who was a professor of psychology at the University of San Francisco and asked him to see me. I asked Warren if he thought I was crazy, and he assured me that he didn't think that at all, but that he thought I should see a doctor that had no involvement with UFOs or anything related. He felt this doctor might be able to help me deal with everything. As I was driving home across the Golden Gate Bridge after my meeting with Warren, I actually considered getting out of my car and jumping. Maybe if I jumped, I could finally put an end to this nightmare. My religious beliefs that suicide is a sin was really what prevented me from resorting to those drastic means that day.

Chapter 21
Psychologist

I decided to do a little research on the doctor that Warren wanted me to visit. I was a little skeptical, because I didn't want to get involved with another character like Tom Jolie. Dr. Hatcher checked out to be a very high powered, well-respected man, who was a hostage and terrorist negotiator, as well as a deprogrammer. He had deprogramed the Iranian hostages when they were released, and he also worked with the survivors from the Jones Town massacre. I called Dr. Hatcher's office, explaining to his secretary that Warren Hinkle had referred me. Dr. Hatcher took my call and said he had expected to hear from me. He told me that Warren briefed him on my situation, and that he would like to schedule an appointment. With some trepidation, I scheduled an appointment for the following week, hoping that this expert could give me some answers, because I knew that I was nearing the end of my rope.

Dr. Hatcher was much younger than I had anticipated. He began my session by telling me that he wanted to see me four times and then he would give me an evaluation. "What's he going to evaluate?" I thought to myself. I decided it didn't really matter, because I was already there and desperately wanted some answers. I began telling him what had happened to me, but he asked me to begin with my childhood. I told him the basics about growing up in San Francisco in a middle class neighborhood with my mother and stepfather. After my fourth session, Dr.Hatcher told me that he wanted to continue to see me, because he felt that I might have a rare form of telekinesis. I asked him to please explain, and he told me that telekinesis was the ability to make things happen. Well, that's a new one, I thought to myself. Let's see now; first it's Satan, then aliens and now telekinesis. At least this was a little less threatening. I began seeing Dr. Hatcher twice a week, and it seemed to be helping just to talk to someone.

Chapter 22
The Hillside

I was working the night shift at the paper, and all of my carriers had shown up except Bill. I called his house to check on him, and his roommate informed me that he had just left. I asked if he had overslept, and the roommate said no, that something or someone was prowling around in their backyard. He said that they were too scared to go out and check it out, but that it sounded like there were two of whatever it was. Just then Bill walked in, so his roommate put him on the phone, and I asked him if he had any idea what had been in his yard. His answer was no. He was running late, so I didn't pursue our conversation. Later on, I went out for coffee with a friend of mine, and when I told him about my conversation with Bill's roommate, we decided to drive over to Bill's house to take a look around. He lived out in a remote area of China Camp in Marin County. The sun was just coming up as we parked the car in from of Bill's house, and we saw Bill's roommate standing beside the house peeking into the back yard. "What are you doing here, John?" he whispered. I asked him if whatever they heard was still around, and he said he didn't know, but that after he and I talked, he heard the same noises in the back. He waited until the sun came up to check it out. I asked him if he was alone, and he said his girlfriend was in the house, but that she wasn't about to come out. Jerry and I followed Bill into the back yard, and I noticed that the tall grass had been trampled. I remarked that whatever it was must have been quite heavy. As we were looking for more clues, Jerry called our attention to something he found on the ground. It looked like a strip of fur, and as I turned it over, I realized that there was flesh on the bottom side. None of us could imagine what kind of animal it would have come from. I asked Bill's roommate for a plastic bag, so that I could take it to a friend of mine who worked in the county sheriff's crime lab, and he obliged by running into the house to get one for me. I asked Jerry if he wanted to accompany me to the lab, but he declined by saying he had things to do.

When I arrived at the sheriff's office, I asked for my friend who worked there and was informed that it was his day off. I dropped the baggy on the desk and asked the officer what he thought it was. He was a little startled and then said that I needed to take it to the SPCA.

On the way to the SPCA, I decided that I would stop by the local newspaper office to see the editor, who was a friend of mine. When I dropped the baggy on his desk, he got a rather horrified look on his face and wanted to know what was in the bag. I told him what happened, and that I was on my way to the SPCA to try and find out exactly what it was. He told me to get it out of there, and he sent one of his reporters with me. My friend knew about my encounter, and his paper did a story about me winning the airplane, so I guess he decided to send someone with me just in case there was another story here. While we were waiting to be helped at the SPCA, I told the reporter what had happened. A gentleman, who was also waiting, said he was going to hang around just to see if I had a piece of ET. We were chuckling over that, when I was called to the counter. When I showed the girl the contents of the baggy and asked her what she thought it was, she said she didn't know. She had someone else take a look, and they agreed that I should take it to Lt. Wilson at the Department of Fish and Game. I asked for his number and called him right away, but I was informed that it was his day off. I left a message asking him to call me as soon as possible, and I told the reporter that I would contact her as soon as I heard anything.

The next day, Lt. Wilson called me and arranged to come over to my house. He looked over the furry piece, and he said he couldn't be completely sure, but he thought it may have come from the neck of a deer that a mountain lion had possibly attacked. I told him that I didn't know that there were mountain lions wandering around the hills in Marin, but he informed me that a few had been spotted from time to time. I still wasn't satisfied. I asked him why we didn't find the carcass of a deer, and he explained that normally the mountain lion will cover their kill with leaves. I thanked him for stopping by, and after he left, I returned to Bill's house to take another look around.

I decided I would thoroughly search the area surrounding the house for a carcass, so I could put this to rest. As I was combing the hillside, I heard rustling in the bushes above me, and when I looked up, I saw several birds fly out of the bushes. I turned away and resumed my search, and again I heard rustling. I turned toward the bushes again, and I froze. There in the bush, looking straight at me was a face. It wasn't like any face I had ever seen. The first thing that went through my mind was, oh my God, they have me! I literally ran backwards. I don't even remember how I got over the fence. I raced to the sheriff's station and ran inside, demanding to see whoever was in charge. They could tell I was obviously very disturbed about something, so I explained that I had just seen something on the hillside that was not human.

The lieutenant asked me what it looked like, and the only way that I could describe it was that it looked kind of like a Kabuki mask. It was white and had very defined features, but it was as if it had no body. After the lieutenant listened to my story, he told me to go downstairs and his deputies would go with me back to the hillside, and he then got on the phone and had three units dispatched to go check it all out. As I was sitting in the back seat of one of the cars on the way to the hillside, I couldn't help but wonder if they didn't all think I was a real nut case. All of the deputies searched the hillside for about half an hour and couldn't come up with anything, and they were looking at me like I must have been hallucinating. They called the lieutenant and told him they came up with a few pot plants, but nothing else. I was so terribly embarrassed. I apologized to them and tried to assure them that I didn't imagine it---something had definitely been there earlier.

I called Dr. Harder that evening and told him what had happened. He asked me a few questions and acted as if he knew exactly what I was talking about. After I hung up the phone, I kept wondered once again if I was going crazy or was something playing games with me? I didn't know what to think anymore.

Chapter 22
Fire

I was working the morning shift, which was 1:30 a.m. to 9:00 a.m. I called in for my messages at 7:00 a.m., and the dispatcher told me that my boss wanted to talk to me. I wondered what that was about, as Terry usually didn't even arrive until after 9:00. I called his office right away, and he told me he had some bad news for me. I was holding my breath. Oh no, what now, I thought to myself. He told me that my car was gone. "Gone? What do you mean gone?" I asked. He told me that my car had caught on fire and burned up. I told him I would be right there. I jumped in the company vehicle, and I don't remember stopping for one traffic light on the way to the office. As I pulled up, the firemen were just leaving. I couldn't believe it. The car I had bought just a couple of months before was now a charred wreck. I walked over to look at it, and my boss came out and told me he was sorry. He said the firemen couldn't figure out what had caused the fire. The heat was so intense it melted the engine block. I looked at what used to be the engine compartment, and my engine was a molten mass. It was incredible. I called Fred and told him to come over and take a look at my car, and he came right away. I called Dr. Harder, and his response was that they had zapped me. "Who zapped me?" I asked. "Aliens" he replied. I told him I would call him later and hung up. What does he mean aliens zapped me, I thought to myself? Next, I called my insurance company. I asked them to check the car out to try to find where the fire originated and what caused it to ignite. I knew an insurance adjuster would go over it with a fine tooth comb and come to a reasonable conclusion. That would put to rest Dr. Harder's claim of alien intervention. A few days went by before I heard from my insurance company. They informed me that their best investigator was assigned to the case, and he was unable to determine what caused the fire. The good news was that they would pay the claim. Interestingly enough, nothing would grow in the dirt area in front of where my car was parked for years to come. At my next session with Dr. Hatcher, I told him about my car burning up, and I asked him if he thought all of these things were just coincidence. His reply was that he wasn't sure.

Years later, I was having lunch with an executive at the paper, and we were talking about my car burning up. He said he believed everything I told him, because he saw the fire department's report, and he had to do a double take when he noticed that the report stated the fire was due to super natural causes.

Chapter 23
Fire

My old boss, Herb, called me from Los Angeles to ask me to do a job for him. I asked him what he needed me to do, as I was barely able to do the job I had, and I was certain I couldn't take on anything else. He told me all he needed me to do was to check on whether there was another company like his in the Santa Rosa area. I figured I could handle that, so I drove up to Santa Rosa to check it out for him. It turned out there was another company in Santa Rosa, so I got their address and went to the office. I posed as someone looking for work and gave the receptionist my name and phone number. That night I received a call from the owner of the company, and we arranged to meet for lunch the next day. He introduced himself as Bill, and he told me he knew who I was. I wondered what he meant by that---had he heard about my UFO experience, or was he just another person trying to get to me. He told me that for years he had heard that John Clark was the best in the business. As it turned out, he used to work for Herb. He laid a thousand dollars on the table and told me it was mine if I would be his partner. I didn't know what to say at first, but finally, I told him that I wasn't interested in traveling anymore. He told me not to worry, because it wouldn't be like working for Herb, since we'd be partners. The offer was certainly tempting. I knew Herb made a lot of money, and I was the one who made it for him. I knew Bill was thinking the same thing, and he was willing to do something about it. I'm not sure exactly why, but I told him that he had a deal. I guess I thought that maybe a change would do me good. At my next session with Dr. Hatcher, I told him how excited I was about starting the new business, and he was very encouraging.

I was very busy during this time, because while we were trying to get the business off the ground, I needed to keep my other job. One day, I received a call from Bill asking me if I could take him to the doctor. It was raining quite hard that afternoon, and he explained that he didn't feel well enough to drive himself. So, I gladly drove him to the doctor's office and read magazines in the waiting room until he was finished. When he came out, I questioned him as to what the doctor felt the problem was, and he told me that they wanted him to go to the hospital for some tests. I said I had noticed lately that it seemed as though he had lost a good deal of weight, and he admitted that he had. The next day, I drove him to the hospital, and when I picked him up, I asked him if the tests had been able to provide any answers. He told me to forget it, but I was persistent and finally was able to get him to confess that the doctor had told him he had cancer of the esophagus and only had about six months to live. We talked at length about what he was thinking and feeling, and I tried very hard to bolster his spirits. However, my words of encouragement seemed to fall on deaf ears, and then I discovered why. He then shared with me the fact that his mother had gone through the same thing, and he knew, therefore, just how bad it would be towards the end. He asked if I would please loan him a shotgun, so that he could end it all right away and spare his family the horror of seeing him suffer and waste away as his mother had. As difficult as it was to do, I had to tell him that I couldn't do that. It dawned on me then that the psychics at the Psychic Institute had said that I had the power to cure or to kill, and I started to get sick to my stomach. I told Bill that I had an appointment and went straight to Dr. Hatcher's house to tell him about Bill's illness

ask him if there was any way he could help me deal with yet another horrible situation. He told me that we couldn't stop anything until we knew what or whom we were dealing with, but that wasn't the answer I wanted to hear.

I was truly at my wit's end. I decided to go to the Embarcadero Center, because they were having a street party, and I thought perhaps it would help take my mind off of everything for a while. But as I walked by a drug store, I remembered that I had heard one time about someone committing suicide by taking aspirin. My thoughts began whirling around in my head, and as ashamed as I am to admit it now, I came to the conclusion that I had better end my life if there was any possibility that I was the cause of people getting sick and maybe even dying. I went into the drug store and bought a bottle of aspirin, and then I went into a bar and ordered drink to wash them down. After I downed them, I saw a friend of mine by the name of Remo. I guess I must have looked a little strange, because he asked me if I was okay. I told him that I was fine, but I was actually starting to feel very weird, and I was beginning to think that maybe I had made a mistake by taking the aspirin. I excused myself and went to the phone to call Dr. Hatcher. When I was told he wasn't in, I asked if he could be paged, because this was an emergency. I held on the line for a few minutes before he got to the phone. I told him that I had taken a bottle of aspirin and had washed them down with vodka, and he then described what was going to happen, which was that the aspirin would begin to eat into my stomach and the pain would be unbearable. I started to panic, and then Bill's face flashed before me. When Dr. Hatcher asked me where I was, I wouldn't tell him, and I hung up the phone. I headed for the garage where my car was parked, when suddenly, one of my legs gave out. I started to limp, and I realized that I couldn't make it, and I became enveloped in fear. Somehow, I was able to get to a phone, and I called Dr. Hatcher back and told him that I needed his help. He asked me once again where I was, and within minutes after I told him, two San Francisco police officers drove up and asked me if I was Mr. Lark. I knew that they meant Clark, but I said no, because I was again feeling that I wanted to go through with it after all. I started for the garage again, and then I really started to feel bad. I looked ahead and saw a police unit no more than twenty feet from me. I stumbled to the car and told them my name, and they said they had been looking for me and had instructions to take me to UCSF. One of the officers asked me who I was and why I was so important, and I asked him what he meant by that. They told me that they hadn't received a red alert on an individual before, so I explained to them that it had to do with flying saucers. They turned on the lights and sirens and rushed me to the hospital. When we arrived at the hospital, there was a team of doctors waiting. They put me on a gurney and took me into the emergency room, where they made me drink some very bitter tasting liquid. I asked them what it was, and they told me it was Icapac and charcoal. I then noticed that Dr. Hatcher was in the room. The next thing I knew, they were pumping my stomach, and then they kept me under observation for a while. Later, someone came to see me and asked if I felt that they should keep me hospitalized for a while, to which I responded no, but the doctor came in and told me that they were going to keep me for at least forty-eight hours. I drifted off, and when I awoke, I found myself on the psychiatric ward, which made me feel like Jack Nicholson in One Flew Over the Cuckoo's Nest. Dr. Hatcher came to see me and asked me how I was doing. I told him that I was feeling much better, and that I certainly had no intentions of every pulling a stunt like that again. I asked him again if there was any possible way he could put a stop to all these crazy happenings, but again he replied that that he couldn't do anything until he knew exactly what we were dealing with. He told me that he was going to keep me in the psychiatric ward for a few more days, because he felt that I would be in danger on the outside. I asked him why, and he told me that Bill had died. That news hit me like a ton of bricks. I was hospitalized for a week, the whole time feeling that it was my fault that Bill died. I know it sounds crazy that I would blame myself, but that was the frame of mind I was in at the time. After one week on the ward, I had everyone there convinced that flying

50

saucers did exist, and I even convinced some of the students on the ward. Dr. Hatcher had me tell my story to the students one afternoon. They were all looking at me like I was some great case study, and Dr. Hatcher told me afterwards that one of the students came to his office and told him that she believed me. He said he told her that she should believe me, because it was all true. Hearing those words, from this man I had come to admire and respect, made me feel a whole lot better about myself.

ORSBORN

TV TONIGHT

■ 8 p.m. "Drugs: Why this Plague." This documentary picks up where Saturday's documentary "Drugs: A Plague Upon This Land" dropped the ball. This examines the hows and whys of the epidemic, and — amazingly — offers some optimism, in the form of possible solutions. Channels 7, 11, 13.

■ 8 p.m. "ALF." Call it, "Throw Dogره from the Train." When ALF is overshadowed by a huggable prop that followed Brian home, he gives it

away to a not-so-lovable woman — played with characteristically nasty flair by "Throw Momma from the Train's" Oscar-nominee Anne Ramsey. Grrrr. Channels 3, 4.

■ 10-30 p.m. "NewPoint." UFOs. Some people say they've seen them. Some say they're just seeing things. John Clark of San Rafael says he not only saw one, but was abducted and taken aboard a UFO in 1975 in the Sequoia National Forest. Joining Clark on the "NewsPoint" hotseat will be UFO expert Dr. James Harter of UC Berkeley. Only the aliens know for sure. Channel 50.

Goldie Hawn in 'Private Benjamin'

For videoph[...]

■ 8 p.m. "Fri[...] (1980). Goldie H[...] as a spoiled rich [...] Army, gets cut d[...] rises above hersel[...] moments. Channe[...]

■ 9 p.m. "The [...] Swansea" (1987) [...] U.S. Olympic biat[...] 1984 by father-an[...] mountain men wh[...] Joe Don Baker do[...] Scary stuff. Chann[...]

For complete listing

arth moves, and ponders

DREAMING on the sofa in writing room, I absent-mi[...] noted that a glass bed [...]

Greenbrae man wins airplane

FEB 20 1981

A slightly dazed Greenbrae man, who has had a pilot's license for 10 years but no plane, won a $46,000 Cessna Skyhawk I early this morning in a Tahoe gaming event.

The winner was John Clark 4? who rt three 25-cent slot machine at 2:30 a.m. to win the grand prize), a special competition at Caesar's since at South Lake Tahoe, according to

Phil Weidinger, publicist for the casino. He said Clark, who was accompanied by his _____, came up with the winning three triple bars to win the plane, which has been hanging from the ceiling for more than three months.

Weidinger said Clark "was somewhat dazed" by his good fortune and said he hadn't decided whether to take the plane or cash.

However, according to Weidinger, Clark, who works for the San Francisco Chronicle's circulation department, has been flying since 1970 but said he didn't own a plane.

Weidinger said the casino had planned to give two of the planes away in a special promotion and a woman won one in December. However, he said, she took cash instead of the aircraft.

03 JUN 1986

John Clark
18 Ninestone Ct.
San Rafael, CA 94903

Dear Mr. Clark:

Your letter of 19 May 1986 requesting documents under the provisions of the Freedom of Information Act has been received in the office of the Information and Privacy Coordinator and has been assigned Reference No. F86-0613 for identification purposes.

Specifically, you have asked for any information on "The Illuminatti." This topic has been the subject of previous requests and, pursuant to diligent searches, we were unable to identify any information or record indexed or filed under such topic. For your information, search costs for the previous request amounted to $164.50.

This concludes our action on your request. Thank you for your interest in the Central Intelligence Agency.

Sincerely,

Lee S. Strickland
Information and Privacy Coordinator

July 3, 1974

156

RE: COUNCIL ON FOREIGN RELATIONS
CINEMA EDUCATIONAL GUILD, INCORPORATED

The Council on Foreign Relations (CFR), 58 East 68th Street, New York, New York, was established in 1922 and is an organization whose membership is made up of prominent men of different professions with various interests and views. It is nonpartisan and noncommercial and membership is restricted to citizens of the United States and by invitation only. Members are chosen chiefly because of knowledge of foreign affairs and daily responsibilities in connection therewith. The organization provides continous conferences on international questions affecting the United States, bringing together experts on state, finance, industry, education, and science in order to create international thought among the peoples of the United States. It publishes "Foreign Affairs," a quarterly whose editor in 1972 was Hamilton Fish Armstrong who, in 1944, was Assistant to the United States Ambassador in London. (u)

The CFR has been the target of attacks by persons who might be politically characterized as "right wing." For example, there is attached a copy of an article which appeared about

London (Enclosure)

OPTIONAL FORM NO. 10

UNITED STATES GOVERNMENT

Memorandum

TO   :   DIRECTOR, FBI   DATE: 12-3

FROM   :   SAC, LOS ANGELES (62-New)

SUBJECT :   ILLUMINATI
            INFORMATION CONCERNING

        Enclosed for the Bureau are five copies of
a letterhead memorandum concerning captioned
organization, submitted in view of the implied threat
to the life of President JOHNSON.

        No investigation has been conducted by the
Los Angeles Office and none is contemplated.

REC- 26   62-109075-76

                           JAN 2 1964

2 - Bureau (Enclosure)(REGISTERED)
1 - Los Angeles
LJM:mak
(3)

Ben Kenobi and the Man With a Dark Secret

By Warren Hinckle

are 320.

Homicide investigation Training Sgt. Rodney Englert of the Multnomah County Division of Public Safety in Portland, Ore., will conduct the seminar.

Englert will cover critical review and

attend.

The two-day seminar will be held in Harrah's Convention Center starting each morning at 8:30 and ending at 4:30 p.m.

For more information, call Pierini at 588-3511.

Waitress reports $250 robbery

A casino cocktail waitress was robbed of $250 early Thursday morning in a Stateline casino parking lot, Douglas County sheriff's officers reported today.

Police said Joyce Marie Hawkins, 25, of South Lake Tahoe, was walking

toward her car about 3 a.m. when a black male adult between ages 20-25, about 6 feet tall with a slender build, approached her from behind.

He grabbed her purse, took out the wallet and fled on foot, police said.

Man wins airplane

The second of two Cessna Skyhawk II airplanes was won at Caesars Tahoe early this morning by a Bay Area resident, a casino spokesman said.

John Clark, 40, of Greenbrae won the plane at 2:30 a.m. after playing only $5 in quarters.

He just got that triple bar, triple bar, triple bar across that lucky bottom line," casino spokesman Phil Weidenger said.

Clark is the circulation manager for the San Francisco Chronicle and has been a pilot since 1970.

Free lessons go along with the single-engine, four-passenger airplane and Clark said he will use the lessons as a refresher course

On the drive up to Tahoe, Clark had premonitions about the plane, saying to his wife they should have rented a plane and flown up and that he felt "lucky tonight."

Obituary

Menditto

Services were held in mid-January in East Haven, Conn. for Michael Menditto, 57, who died Jan. 19 in Ft. Lauderdale, Fla.

A former 15-year South Lake Tahoe resident, Menditto had been a prominent show business musician.

Born July 4, 1923 in New Haven, he was the son of the late Nicola and Josephine Agone Menditto. He attended local schools and the Yale University School of Music. While in high school he had his own show on a New Haven radio station.

Menditto appeared in theaters in New York including the Capitol, Paramount, Strand and Apollo, as well as the Astor Hotel. He played in orchestras conducted by Hugo Winterhaulter, Shelly Manne and Dizzy Gillespie.

World War II, serving in the Army Band and later formed his own show entertaining troops. After the war, he moved to California and played with several bands, including Alvin Rey and Del Courtney.

Menditto worked a number of years at Harrah's Club until 1969 when he joined the Henry Mancini orchestra. He also had worked on several large cruise ships. In 1977 he moved to Hawaii where he was employed at the Hyatt Regency Hotel in Honolulu.

He is survived by his wife, Analiss Saal Menditto of Germany, two daughters, Michele Hock of Sacramento and Sharel Wilson of South Lake Tahoe; a son, Rick Menditto of South Lake Tahoe; a sister, Mary Citerella of East Haven; two nieces:

Chapter 24
Television Interview

I had many messages waiting for me upon return home from the hospital, and one of them was from the television show Evening Magazine. At that time, it was one of my favorite programs, with Richard Hart and Jan Yanahero acting as the co-hosts of the show. I immediately called the television station and asked to speak to Richard Hart. I explained to him who I was, and he told me that he had read Warren Hinkle's article and wanted to do a story about my experiences. He also mentioned that he saw me on television after I had won the airplane, and that he, too, was a pilot and a UFO buff. He asked me if Evening Magazine could come out to my house and film a segment about my story. I didn't want to tell him that I had just returned from the hospital, but I did ask for a little time to think it over. He said that would be fine and to call him back in a few days. I called Dr. Hatcher and asked him what he thought about my doing a segment for the program. He knew of Richard Hart and said he thought he was a professional and wouldn't do anything to hurt or embarrass me. He left the decision up to me as to whether I felt I was up to another interview and if I thought anything good would come of it. I thanked him for his time and told him I would let him know what I decided. The first thing that came to mind was the other television show I appeared on with Dr. Harder and how frightened I had been. However, I felt that this would be different, since they would be filming it at my home, and that I probably wouldn't feel quite so intimidated doing the interview in familiar surroundings. I was still hoping that someone would hear about my experiences and be able to give me some of the answers I was seeking, and I felt that perhaps this program could be the impetus to do just that. So, I called Richard the next day and told him I would do the show, as long as they agreed to film at my home. He assured me that it would be absolutely no problem to tape the segment there, and we went ahead and set the date.

While the crew from Evening Magazine was setting up their equipment to tape the segment, I struck up a conversation with the cameraman. It turned out that he was really into flying saucers, and he shared all kinds of great information with me. I told him about the Ouija Board, and how it mentioned Rah and the Illuminati, and he said that the Illuminati was comprised of aliens, which was exactly what the

Ouija Board had said also. We had to wrap up our conversation, because everyone was ready to begin filming. The taping went better than I anticipated. I actually enjoyed doing it and had positive feelings about the response it may provide.

Chapter 25
The Illuminati

A few days later, I asked my boss at the newspaper if I could go to the morgue, which is newspaper jargon for the section where old newspaper articles are filed according to subject matter. He told me he would check on it and get back to me. He was so supportive of me through all of this, and I've always felt I probably wouldn't have been able to hold on to my job if it hadn't been for him. He called me back right away and told me I could go ahead and use the morgue, and he wished me luck in finding whatever it was I was searching for. I couldn't wait to pull the file on Sirhan. Rumor had it that his notebook had supposedly disappeared, and in his notebook, there was a reference to the Illuminati. I didn't really expect to find anything, but it was the only lead I had. As I was going through the file, I noticed that I was being watched with great interest by someone else in the room. At first I thought he was just a reporter doing research, but then, after realizing how much he was actually watching me, I began to wonder just who he really was and what he was up to. I decided to try to ignore him and went back to my search. I came across a small article mentioning that Sirhan was a member of the Rosacrutions, and I vaguely recalled seeing that name somewhere before, but I just couldn't remember where. I put the file back and decided I would call Dr. Haines and tell him what I had uncovered. When I talked to him, I asked him if he had ever heard of the Rosacrutions, but he was very vague and implied that he really didn't know anything about them. I told him that I had researched them rather extensively and when I found out that their headquarters were in San Jose, I decided that I would go down and check it out. He wished me luck, and I was on my way to San Jose.

I parked in front the Rosacrutions headquarters and was struck by the Egyptian architecture. I remembered what the Ouija Board had said about Rah my having been at war with Rah. Rah was an Egyptian Sun God, and these buildings, with their Egyptian appearance, suddenly took on new meaning for me. I didn't know if I had the courage to walk into them or not. I decided I needed the information, and like it or not, this was something I had to do. I walked up to the reception desk and told the woman I was interested in becoming a member of their organization, and she asked me to have a seat and said she would send someone out to talk to me. I still do not know how I kept from bolting from the room, because the fear I was feeling was nearly overwhelming. A little old lady came out to greet me, and once I saw her, I told myself to calm down, because this was obviously not going to be a big deal. She explained to me what I would need to do to become a member, and I then summoned the courage to ask her where the Illuminati fit into their organization. I thought this might cause her to become alarmed, as if I knew some great secret, but, without hesitation, she said that the Illuminati was the upper echelon. I couldn't believe my ears! I looked over my shoulder to make sure I had an easy escape route. Next, I asked her if she had any information she could give me on the Illuminati, and she simply told me to meet her in the temple, and she would be able to talk to me there. I asked for directions, and she instructed me to go outside and come in through the temple's outside entrance.

A few minutes later, I was at the doors to the temple and was awed by the enormity of them. They were wide open, and there were two very large men, who appeared to be of Middle Eastern descent, standing guard. As I attempted to enter the temple, they stopped me and asked where I was headed. I told them about the woman I had met with, and that she had instructed me to meet her in the temple. While I was explaining this to them, the woman entered from the other side of the temple, and I pointed her out to them. One of the guards walked over to talk to her. They were out of my earshot, but he seemed to be very upset. The woman, obviously shaken, came over and took me by the arm and walked me to the street. "Meet me in the rose garden in an hour", she whispered to me. I asked her where the rose garden was located, and she told me not to worry, because I would have no difficulty finding it. She turned and hurried back into the temple, at which point I began to wonder what was going on and what I was getting myself into. It was beginning to look like maybe I should let all of this go, get into my car and drive home, but I had come this far, and maybe, just maybe, I was on to something. Anyway, I had an hour to think it over.

Walking into the metaphysical bookstore across the street from the temple, I noticed that the clerk, who had been conversing with a customer, stopped talking as soon as I came in, but then I told myself that I'm probably just being paranoid. I decided to browse around and see if I could find anything on the Illuminati. When the customer left the store, I asked the clerk if they had anything on the Illuminati, and she told me that they had nothing on that topic. I told her that it was my understanding that the Illuminati was the upper echelon of the Rosacrutions, to which she responded that I was correct and that they were still active. I asked her if there was anything else she could tell me about the Illuminati, and she asked me how I found out about it. I told her about the Ouija Board, and that bit of information seemed to get her attention. She informed me that she was a medium and asked if she could do a reading on me. I agreed. She led me to her office, and she asked me to put my hands out, palms up. She put her hands on mine and immediately removed them. "Oh,` my God!" she exclaimed. "What's wrong?" I asked. She told me it was just that never had she felt energy like mine. My mind wandered back to my session at the Psychic Institute and how they told me the very same thing. The clock on her wall indicated it was time for me to meet the woman in the rose garden. The clerk gave me directions, and, as I was leaving the store, she asked me to try to come back after my meeting, because she might have some information for me. I told her that I would try. The rose garden was deserted when I arrived, so I decided to sit on a bench and wait. I waited for an hour, and the woman didn't show up. I was really disappointed, and I decided to skip going back to the bookstore, because I'd had enough for one day.

At a restaurant on my way home, I struck up a conversation with the man sitting next to me. In talking, I discovered that he was a police officer. He asked me what brought me to San Jose, and I told him the highlights of what had transpired to cause me to be there. He said it was the most incredible story he had ever heard, so I asked him if he would be willing to go undercover to check out the Rosacrutions, and he said he would. I told him that if they were who I thought they were, they would know he was coming. I guess my comment frightened him, because he then dropped the subject of going undercover.

Chapter 26
Sirhan Sirhan

Dr. Hatcher's office was my first stop after returning from San Jose. I told him about my day, and he seemed a little upset that the woman didn't meet me in the rose garden, but he didn't tell me why. I changed the subject by asking him about a flyer I had read in the hallway outside his office. It was a notice of a lecture being given by Dr. Hatcher and a professor by the name of Dr. Diamond. He asked me why I was interested, and I told him that Dr. Diamond's name appeared in Sirhan's file as the psychiatrist who evaluated Sirhan for the prosecution, and that I would very much like to talk to him. Dr. Hatcher said I could talk to him right away, because he had just finished having a conversation with him right before I arrived and was probably still in his office. I got directions to Dr. Diamond's office, but I was a little apprehensive as I knocked on the door, because, after all, he didn't know me, and he might end up having me committed to the psychiatric ward. Dr. Diamond was a very distinguished looking man who appeared to be in his sixties. I introduced myself, and he told me he knew who I was, because Dr. Hatcher had phoned him to let him know I was stopping by. He asked me to have a seat, and after I finished relating my experiences to him, up to and including my trip to San Jose, he stunned me by telling me I was on the right trail. I asked him what he meant. He said when he hypnotized Sirhan, he found out that he was in a hypnotic state at the time of the shooting, if, in fact, he actually did do the shooting. He also said, while he was under hypnosis, that he loved Robert Kennedy, but that he didn't like the fact that Kennedy was selling jets to Israel. Dr. Diamond told me that this fact alone was not enough motivation for Sirhan to kill Robert Kennedy, but it was enough for programming purposes. Afterwards, Dr. Diamond found out that Sirhan was a member of the Rosacrutions, and in following up on that organization, he learned of the Illuminati. He told me that every lead he followed about the Illuminati turned into a brick wall. He said that there was a missing link somewhere, and that the only other case he had worked on similar to this was the Charles Manson case. I told Dr. Diamond that I knew Tex Watson. He was curious as to how I knew him, and I explained that I had met him at a party when I lived in Hollywood. Tex and a friend of his had offered me some acid at that party, and I declined.

We got to talking about various things, and somewhere during our conversation, Tex mentioned that he'd never been in snow. I asked them if they had ever been up to the San Bernardino Mountains, and they told me they had not, so I asked them if they'd like to take a drive up there to Big Bear, where there was snow. They liked that idea, and, on the way back, they invited me to go out to the ranch with them. I told them I couldn't go, because I had to leave for a business trip the next day, but I would go with them when I returned. I was in New York when I saw the headline "Sharon Tate Killed." When I found out later that Tex had been the murderer, I was horrified, because I remembered that drive to the mountains with Tex in the back seat of my car. I certainly was glad that I didn't go out to the ranch. I told Dr. Diamond that I might be able to talk to Tex if he remembered me, and I could ask him if he knew anything about the Rosacrutions and the Illuminati, and he told me he would appreciate any information I could obtain. He thought that maybe, because I wasn't part of the "establishment", Tex might open up to me, so I said I'd give it a shot. I asked Dr. Diamond if he thought it was a little strange that I started out discussing flying saucers and now I was talking to him about Charles Manson and Tex Watson. I also asked him if he felt we were dealing with super natural forces, but he said he wouldn't go so far as to say that. I asked him if he could give me any other explanation, and he said that he could not, so I thanked him for his time, and he wished me luck.

Chapter 27
Rosacrutions

I called Dr. Haines to fill him in on my trip to the Rosacrutions and their connection to the Illuminati, and I also told him about my conversation with Dr. Diamond. He asked me if he could see me at my house, and we made arrangements to meet the following Saturday. Dr. Haines brought his wife along with him, and since it was a beautiful day, we all sat around the pool. I reiterated as to what I had been able to find out about the Rosacrutions and their connection to the Illuminati, and he turned to his wife and said "See, I told you so." I thought to myself, wait a minute, Dr. Haines told me he didn't know anything about the Rosacrutions. He interrupted my thoughts by telling me to be please be careful, because they can get violent. Oh great, that was just what I needed to hear. Not only is he confirming that the Illuminati does exist, but also that they may get violent. For some strange reason, however, I didn't believe that I was in any danger. After all, if they were as powerful as my investigation led me to believe, they could easily discredit me as some UFO nut. I said goodbye to Dr. Haines and his wife and thanked them for coming.

Chapter 28
The Russian Consulate

I had seen just about every top expert there was, and I still had no answers. I read something in the paper about the Russians researching UFOs and other paranormal, so I decided to talk to them. I went to the Russian consulate in San Francisco on Green Street and found the building looked rather foreboding, with the security cameras coming at me from every angle. I walked past it a couple of times, before I finally decided to ring the bell. I felt as though I were entering another world. It was so cold inside that I thought maybe they hadn't paid their heating bill, or perhaps they just wanted to feel at home. I went to the counter to see if there was someone I could talk to about their UFO research. The man behind the glass partition told me that the person I would need to talk to was in Moscow, and he would be back in a week, so I set up an appointment for the following Thursday. When I arrived at the consulate for the scheduled appointment, they buzzed me right in. A very large man opened the door, and it brought back memories of the day I visited the Rosacrutions. "Come in Mr. Clark" he said, and he told me to take a seat on the bench. A short while later, a gentleman came out and asked how he could help me. I told him that I was being tested for telekinesis, and that there was a possibility that I had been abducted. I went on to say that it was my understanding that they were doing a vast amount of research on UFOs, and I would be willing to go to Moscow and let them test me. He asked me what I wanted in exchange, and I said I wanted any information they could give me on the assassination of Robert Kennedy and also about the Illuminati. Seconds later, there was a slight tap on the plate glass window behind me. The man I was talking with abruptly ended our conversation, and the next thing I knew I was being escorted out of the building.

From the consulate, I went to Dr. Hatcher's office, since it was fairly close by. I told him where I had been and what transpired. He was furious with me. Never before had I seen him lose his cool like he did then. He asked me if I realized that they could have kept me, because, after all, I was on their turf. I told him that I hadn't thought of that, but that I was certainly willing to take the risk in order to get the information I was looking for. He calmed down somewhat, but he asked me to promise him that I would not return to the consulate. I agreed to that, because I knew I wouldn't be able to go back there anyway. After leaving his office, I started to wonder just why he had been so upset. A couple of days later, I found out. I was talking with a reporter friend of mine, and I asked him if he knew for a fact that the name Illuminati appeared in Sirhan's notebook and if the notebook had actually disappeared. He said that as far as he knew, the name Illuminati did not appear in any note-book. I told him about the Russian consulate and Dr. Hatcher's response. He looked surprised and asked me if I was talking about Chris Hatcher, and I told him that I was. I asked him why he was so surprised. "He works for the CIA" he responded. It was as if someone punched me in the stomach. I had trusted Dr. Hatcher, and I had told him everything. I was devastated. I was really beginning to believe that there was nobody out there who would be able to help me. I didn't know where to turn or who to trust.

Chapter 29
Tex Watson

After contemplating about all of the people I had come in contact with since my encounter in Sequoia and everything that happened to me afterwards, I decided that, like it or not, I would not be able to rest until I followed every lead. After giving it a good deal of thought, I decided to try to contact Sirhan by writing to him through his lawyer, but I wasn't too surprised when I didn't receive any response. I tried Tex Watson, because I thought there was a chance he might remember me. I was correct! Tex did remember me, and he wrote back right away. I contacted the prison system to inquire about obtaining permission to visit him, and I was told that as long as the prisoner said it was okay for me to visit, I was welcome.

As I was driving into the California Men's Colony, I was thinking about how Tex looked the last time I saw him, and what it would be like to meet with him under these circumstances. I went to the office and told the guard on duty that I was there to see Tex Watson. The guard brought him outside, and Tex suggested that we sit at one of the picnic tables. As we sat down, I remembered the picnic bench I had slept on in Sequoia. A strange feeling was coming over me as I thought about the fact that I was sitting down to chat with a mass murderer. We talked a bit about the day we met, and then I got down to the real reason I came to see him. I asked him if he had ever heard of the Rosacrutions. He thought they were some type of religious organization, but he didn't know anything about them, so I asked him if he had heard of the Illuminati, to which he answered no. We then talked about how he was doing, and he told me that he had become an ordained minister, and also that he had gotten married since he had been in prison and now had two children. I must admit that I was rather surprised that someone imprisoned for murder would be allowed not only to marry, but to father children as well. I asked him why he killed all of those innocent people, especially a pregnant woman (Sharon Tate). He told me that he didn't want to kill her, and that she had pleaded with him to let her live, at least until she had her baby, and that then he could do what he wanted with her. He had decided to spare her, but one of the girls who was with him yelled at him to kill her, and she said that if he didn't, she would tell Charlie. He said then it was like a dream, and he started stabbing Sharon Tate.

I asked him if he was stoned at the time, and he told me that he had been. I asked him how he could go on to kill the La Biancas after thinking about what he had done to Sharon Tate, but he said he didn't have an answer for that. I asked him what Charles Manson was like. "He's possessed." was his reply, and I urged him to explain. "He's possessed by the devil." he answered, and he went on to say that "Manson enjoys being Manson, and if he were let out, he would probably do the same thing." "What about you?" I asked. "I would like to ride off into the sunset, with the hope that everyone would forget about me, and I wish that all the families of the victims could somehow find it in their hearts to forgive me for what I have done." he replied. I realized Tex didn't have any information that would help me, so I decided to wrap up my visit. Before I left, I asked him if he could write a letter for me to give to Charles Manson so that I might be able to get in at Vacaville, where he was then being held, to see him. Tex went ahead and wrote the letter for me, telling Manson that it was okay to talk to me. I thanked him for his time and headed home.

Chapter 30
Lake Tahoe

One day, I was having a bite to eat at a restaurant near my home, when I struck up a conversation with the man sitting next to me. I told him I was going to go to Vacaville to see Charles Manson, and he suggested to me that I had better clear it with the SSU first. "Who's the SSU? I asked. He said they were the special security unit for the prison system. They were people who went after escaped prisoners and parole jumpers. He went on to say that one time these guys caught an escapee working at a car wash, and they put him face down on the ground and blew him away. I asked him how I could contact them, and he said he wasn't sure, so I asked him where he got this information. "I was in the joint." he responded. He had been in Vacaville with Manson, and he even knew his cell number, which later checked out to be true. We started talking about other things, and I told him about my winning the airplane in Tahoe with the UFO hovering over the casino. He then told me that Jacques Cousteau had been denied access to Lake Tahoe, which he found out from a friend of his who owned a marina in Tahoe and who was also a friend of Cousteau. Apparently Cousteau wanted to take a mini-submarine and explore the bottom of Lake Tahoe, and since the average depth was 800 ft. and the deepest was 1200 ft., a submarine would be the only way he would be able to explore it. He went on to explain that there was a lot of folklore surrounding the Lake, which I asked him to explain. He told me that after the railroads were built, they killed the coolies and dumped the bodies in the Lake. Supposedly it was used as a dumping ground for the Mafia and the CIA disposing of bodies, as well. "If that's true, the bottom of the lake must look like a grave yard, but what I don't understand is why the bodies don't float to the top", I interjected. He said they didn't float because of the altitude and the temperature of the lake, but that there was one story of a woman's body washing up on one of the beaches, and that she was in period clothes and was perfectly preserved. His last statement really caught my attention. He said many people have reported seeing flying saucers coming out of the lake, and that was something I most certainly had never heard before.

Chapter 31
Jacques Cousteau

I thought about what the man at the restaurant had told me about Lake Tahoe and decided to take a drive up there to see what I could find out. The first place I visited was Caesar's. It was my first time back since winning the plane, and I immediately went over to the slot machine that I had won the plane on. I was rather surprised to find that they had put a plaque on it noting the fact that I had won the plane, the date I won and my hometown. I put in three quarters, pulled the handle and . . . nothing. Oh well, I wasn't here to gamble anyway.

I parked at the marina, asked for the owner and introduced myself to him. I asked him if he had a moment, as I wanted to ask him a few questions. I'm sure he thought I was going to ask him about fishing, but instead I told him it was my understanding that he was a friend of Jacques Cousteau. "What's it to ya?" he asked, somewhat on the defensive. I told him not to worry, because I wasn't a reporter or a cop, and that I was just curious as to why Cousteau was denied access to the lake. He still didn't seem to be warming up to me, so I changed the subject and told him about my winning the airplane. He remembered reading about me in the paper and said he wished he had won, because he, too, was a pilot. We had developed a bit of camaraderie, it seemed, so he then told me that it was true Cousteau had been denied access, and that he could never understand why they wouldn't let him into the lake, since they let everyone else have access. I asked who had the authority to deny him access, and he responded that it was the Federal Government's jurisdiction. He told me that the San Jose Mercury News had a mini-sub in the lake awhile back, and when I asked if they found anything, he said no. Apparently the submarine burned up just as they were starting to go out. My mind raced back to my car burning up, and I asked if they found out why it burned. He said it was suspicious, but that the investigators said it was due to an electrical short in the wiring. He went on to tell me about another time, when a man was on the lake trying to set a world record for speed and his boat flipped, and, according to the media, they couldn't find his body for a couple of days. He said that was nonsense, because he knew the coroner, and he had been at the scene. They found the man's body the same day of the accident by using a remote camera, but it turned out that the picture in the camera was not of the same man. I asked what all of this had to do with Jacques Cousteau, and he told me that it really didn't, but that there were lots of stories about strange happenings on and around the lake. I asked him if he had heard about the woman in period dress washing up on a beach in a perfectly preserved state, and he said that everyone up at the lake had heard that story once or twice. I asked him if he thought it was true, and he said he didn't know, but he gave me the name of a friend of his, Max Bennett, who was at one time the chief of police at North Shore, because he thought Max may be able to give me more information.

Chapter 32
Navy Mini Sub

I stopped at a gas station in North Shore, and since it's a small community, I asked the attendant if he knew where I might find Max Bennett. I guess he thought I needed the police, because he informed me that he had retired from the police force. I explained that I was aware of that, but I wondered if he knew how I could reach him, so he told me he hung out at a local watering hole called Pete & Peter's, and that it was just down the road. When I walked in, everyone turned and looked at me. It was definitely a local bar, and they all were obviously wondering who I was and how I found their favorite spot. I ordered a drink and asked the bartender if he knew Max Bennett. "Who wants to know?" he growled, which made me wonder why so many people in this town seemed to be on the defensive. Did they have something to hide? I told him that I had been talking with Jim Stewart, and that he suggested that I might be able to find Max at Pete & Peter's. The bartender then seemed to relax a bit and asked me if I was a friend of Jim's. "Sort of" I replied. The bartender told me that Max would be in shortly. While I was waiting for him to show up, I began talking to the man sitting next to me. At one time, he was the captain for Bill Harrah's yacht, and now he was the captain of the ferry that operates on Lake Tahoe for tourists. I asked him if he had heard about Jacques Cousteau's request being denied, and he said he had heard something about it. I asked if he had ever seen anything out of the ordinary in his years of traversing the lake, and he told me that one night he almost hit a Navy mini-submarine running on the surface, because apparently the submarine had its running lights turned off. I asked him how he knew it was a Navy submarine, and he replied that he had been in the Navy, and he knew a Navy submarine when he saw one. I heard the door to the bar open, and the bartender said "Hey, Max, how are ya doing? There's someone here looking for you. He says he's a friend of Jim Stewart's." I went over and introduced myself and explained that Jim suggested I talk to him. He asked me what I wanted to talk about, so I began by asking him if he knew why Jacques Cousteau was denied access to Lake Tahoe. He then asked me to join him at a table in the corner, where he asked me why I was so curious about this matter. I didn't want him to think that I was a crackpot, so I told him I was writing a book about the history of Lake Tahoe. My answer appeased him, and he said he always thought it was very strange that they had denied Cousteau access to the lake. I asked him who "they" were, and he said "the Feds." Then I asked if he knew why, and he said he did not. I told him about the gentleman at the bar seeing a mini-submarine running on the surface and asked him if he knew anything about that. He said yes, because it had been reported to the Coast Guard. "Coast Guard, what Coast Guard?" I asked. Max explained that there was a Coast Guard station on North Shore, which really surprised me. He seemed to be a pretty down to earth guy and was easy to talk to, so I decided to continue on with my questions. I asked him about the man who was killed while trying to set the world record for speed on the lake, and I presented the story as Jim had told it to me, with the coroner saying that the video picture was not of the right person. This piqued his interest, and he asked "which coroner was that?" I asked him what he meant. "Which County?" he queried. I told him that I didn't know, and that he would have to find out that information from Jim. I asked him if he knew of anyone was doing any type of research on Lake Tahoe, and he said that Dr. Goldman's team from UC Davis was doing some. We continued to chat about the lake for a while longer, and I thanked him for the information. Before I left, I told him I was the one who had won the airplane at Caesar's. "You're the one! Well, here, let's shake. Maybe some of that will rub off on me." he exclaimed. I certainly hope not, I thought to myself.

Chapter 33
Mysterious Helicopter

My next stop was the Coast Guard station. I asked the guardsman if he had a report on file about the mini-submarine, and he said he would check for me. After searching for some time for the report, he returned to say that it looked like it was no longer in their files. I thought you had to keep all of your files, I said. The guardsman admitted that all the files were kept, but after a certain period of time, they were sent to the archives in Washington, D.C. I asked him if he had ever spotted a mini- submarine on the lake, and he said that he had not. I asked him if he happened to know whether Dr. Goldman from UC Davis had an office in the neighborhood, and he told me Dr. Goldman was working out of a trailer and gave me directions.

The woman behind the desk at the trailer informed me that Dr. Goldman was out at the moment, and she asked if she could be of assistance. I explained that I was interested in the research being done on Lake Tahoe, and I asked her how the lake was created. She said it was caused by a rift zone. I told her that I had thought it was volcanic, because I had read somewhere that the lake was an extinct volcano. She assured me that this was not the case. I asked her the measurement of the deepest part of the Lake, adding that I had heard that it was bottomless. She said the deepest part was 1200 ft., which prompted me to ask her the location of that area, and she told me it was about a mile from where we were. I asked her about the marine life to be found there, and she told me there were crayfish, trout and salmon. I asked her how deep the crayfish went, thinking that since crayfish are scavengers, they would take care of any bodies that were in the lake, and she said that the deepest they were able to ascertain was 600-800 ft. I asked if, in their research, they had ever seen the entire bottom of the lake, and she said they hadn't been able to, because when they put a remote camera down, the strong current pulls it later-ally. I asked her if she thought that a body could stay in a preserved state while being in the water, and she thought this may be possible. I asked her if the researchers had ever seen anything unusual come out of the lake, and she asked me exactly what I was referring to. I decided this would be my last question. "Well, such as a flying saucer. Have the researchers ever seen one come out of the lake?" She looked at me as if I were some kind of lunatic, and she replied icily that she didn't think they had, and that, as I had anticipated, was the end of our conversation.

I stopped for lunch at the South Tahoe Airport on my way home and noticed a very large helicopter with no markings or registration number. I thought that it was really strange, because all aircraft had to be marked with an "N number." I asked the waitress if that helicopter was parked there all the time, and she informed me that it came and went. I asked her if she knew which direction it headed, and she responded that it headed to and from the lake. I thought to myself that if there were a mini-submarine in the lake, the helicopter could be the tool that they use to get it into the water. If they did it at night over the middle of the lake, nobody would be able to see or hear anything. I wasn't sure if any of this information meant anything or if it even pertained to my situation, but I decided it had been a very interesting trip, indeed.

Chapter 34
Charles Manson

I made the arrangements for a meeting with Charles Manson. As I was driving to Vacaville, I marveled at how my investigation had led me down so many different paths, and that here I was on my way to talk to Charles Manson, of all people. I wondered what could possibly come next, and if I would be financially and emotionally able to continue to track every lead. I told myself that, at some point, I would have to give it all up. If only all the bizarre incidents would stop happening to me, maybe I could put it all to rest. I noticed, as I was parking my car in the visitor's area, how foreboding the prison looked----nothing like the Men's Colony where I visited Tex Watson. I told the guard I was there to see Charles Manson. He raised an eyebrow at me, and I produced the clearance I had been issued from the Bureau of Prisons, and I also gave him the letter Tex had written for me. I was escorted into the glass house, which is an area where the prisoner can see the visitor, but the visitor cannot see the prisoner. I had been sitting there for approximately twenty minutes, when I heard someone shouting something. The guard came in, pulled me into a corner where Manson could not see us, and asked me if I was sure I wanted to see him. I assured him that indeed l did, and I asked him if there was a problem. The guard said that Manson thought I wanted to kill him. "Kill him? No, no, no, I just want to talk to him." I replied. I asked the guard if he had given Manson the letter from Tex Watson. He said he had, and that's when Manson started to go berserk. Manson told the guard to tell me that he would see me, but I would need to write to him first. Another hurdle I thought to myself, and I thanked the guard and left. Driving home, I wondered why Manson reacted that way to me, and why would he want me to write to him. What was in the letter from Tex that set him off? I would have to think about whether or not I wanted to pursue this trail any farther. Would it be more trouble and frustration than it was worth?

Chapter 35
Dr. Hatcher Equals CIA

Returning home from Vacaville, I retrieved a message from my answering machine from Dr. Hatcher. He was calling to find out why I had skipped my last two sessions, so I called him and apologized for missing my appointments and explained that I needed to get away for a few days. He asked me where I went, and I told him I went to Lake Tahoe, but I left out the details. I asked him if he had ever heard of the SSU, and he replied that he didn't think he had and wondered why I wanted to know. I told him that I was just curious; that someone had mentioned it to me, and I thought he might know something about it. We made an appointment for me to see him the following week. I decided it might be worth checking out whether or not the SSU really existed, so I began my research once again. Finally, after a lot of hard work, I tracked down the name and telephone number of a contact person for the SSU. I called the man and introduced myself, explaining that I had been told to check with him, and he wondered what I needed to check with him about. I told him that I didn't know whether he knew it or not, but that I had tried to contact Sirhan, that I did visit Tex Watson, and that I had attempted to visit Charles Manson. I also mentioned that I was working with Dr. Hatcher. His reply was, "Oh, Chris? Good man, tell him hello for me. I have no problem with what you're doing." I thanked him and hung up the phone. I couldn't believe it. Why did Dr. Hatcher deny knowing anything about the SSU? The head man just called him by his first name. Why isn't he being straight with me?

Chapter 36
Psychic Syla Brown

    While channel surfing one evening, I come across an interview with a psychic by the name of Sylvia Brown. She was appearing on Evening Magazine, which was the same program I had been on. I liked what she had to say and had a good feeling about her, so I decided to call Richard Hart and ask him for her telephone number. I called her office to arrange for a meeting, but I didn't give them any particulars as to why I wanted to meet with her. When Sylvia and I sat down to talk, I began by asking her if she knew what it was that I had come into contact with in Sequoia. Her response was that it was my spirit guide---very tall and silver. "Why, then, do aliens keep entering into the picture in that was my spitit guide?" I asked. She said that in my previous life, she was seeing me in a flying machine directing the building of the pyramids. It was interesting to me that the Egyptians should be coming up once again. I remembered the Quiji board and what it said about my war with Rah. Sylvia may have seen me on television, but I knew that I had not mentioned the part about Rah when I was on the program. She went on to say that I had a golden triad, but she didn't explain what that meant. She said she didn't have any more time and had to be on her way. I left wondering why Egypt kept entering the picture. It was as if someone had written a script (a very bad one), and I was acting it out.

Chapter 37
Sodium Penathol

In a telephone conversation with Dr. Harder, I asked if it would be possible for him to give me Sodium Penathol. I had done some research into the drug and felt that maybe it could unlock a part of my mind that was closed. He told me that he couldn't get it for me, because he was not a medical doctor. I asked him if he knew of anyone who might be able to get it for me, and he told me to ask Dr. Hatcher. As it happened, I already had an appointment scheduled with Dr. Hatcher for the next day.

As I walked into Dr. Hatcher's office, I realized I had my guard up somewhat. It was the first time I had met with him since my conversation with the man from the SSU. He picked up on my uneasiness and asked me what was wrong, so I decided to confront him. I explained that I had been told that he worked for the CIA, and, without any hesitation, he replied that he had done some work for them in the past, but that he was no longer employed by them. I then told him that Mr. Walsh from the SSU had said to say hello, and he immediately changed the subject. I decided not to pursue the subject at this time. I asked him if he could get Sodium Penathol. He explained how Sodium Penathol worked, and that it had a very narrow window, meaning that if there wasn't enough administered, there wouldn't be a reaction, and if too much was given, I would just blabber about anything. So much for that idea. He then told me that he wanted to put me on some type of medication. I recalled Dr. Harder's warning that "they" would drug me to find out what I knew, so I told Dr. Hatcher that I didn't want him to give me anything, because I didn't want to become dependent on a medication. Not taking no for an answer, he tried to convince me that he could give me something that would help to relieve my anxiety. I told him I would have to think about it, and that ended our session for the day.

Chapter 38
Return Camping Trip

After considerable persuasion, I convinced my brother to accompany me back to the campground in Sequoia. I wanted to see if whatever it was would contact me again. I phoned Dr. Harder and told him of my plans. He said that it didn't really matter, because whatever I came in contact with would be able to find me anywhere, not just in Sequoia. Nonetheless, this was something I wanted to do, so my brother picked me up and we were on our way. During the drive, I kept asking myself if I was doing the right thing. After all, I was returning to the scene where my nightmare began, and even after exhaustive research I still didn't know who or what I was dealing with. I didn't want to discuss my fears with my brother, because, after all, he would be there with me. He had been in Vietnam, and I felt that I could certainly rely on him to help me if anything happened. When we arrived at the ranger station, we were told that the campsite was closed during the winter season. I pleaded with the ranger and told him it was important for us to be able to set up at the campsite. He shrugged his shoulders and told us it would be okay, but we would have to park out on the road and walk in. He also said that we would be the only people in the camp. When that thought registered, my heart sank to my knees. I wondered if I had the courage to go ahead and camp out there overnight. Before I had time to reconsider, we were in the car heading toward the area where we could park. We unpacked our gear, carried it to the campground and set up camp. It was very cold, so we started a fire and sat down near it to stay warm. My brother lit his pipe and sat staring into the flames. After all the years that had passed, I couldn't believe that I was back in this place. In a way, it felt like it had been only yesterday that I took my family on an innocent camping trip that ended up changing my life forever. As darkness fell, I really became frightened. I couldn't remember a time in my life that I was quite this scared, outside of the time the engines quit on the plane in Hawaii. I told my brother that I was going to hit the sack. He said he was going to stay up for a while and read. I knew that he was really standing guard. As I lay in the tent in my sleeping bag, I was constantly watching for shadows on the walls of the tent. This whole scenario reminded me of when I was a child in bed at night, afraid that a monster was going to come and get me. I watched all night.

Every little noise was so amplified that I thought I probably could have heard an ant walking. I couldn't wait for morning to come. This was one time that I would have even welcomed Rah, the Sun God. Eventually, morning did arrive, and I got up to check on my brother. He had stayed up all night outside the tent keeping watch. "Well, nothing happened." he said. I told him that I didn't want to stay there another night and suggested we pack up and go home after breakfast. There was certainly no argument from him. On the way back home, I came to the horrible realization that I probably would never find the answers I was so desperately seeking.

Chapter 39
Surgery

A few months later, I was informed that I would need surgery on my knee. When the scheduled day arrived, I was rolled into the operating room, placed on the operating table, and they began to administer Sodium Penathol. The anesthetist told me to start to count backwards, and the next thing I knew I was waking up in the recovery room. The pain in my leg was nearly unbearable, so I called for the nurse and asked her to give me something for the pain. She told me that she wouldn't be able to give me much, due to all the medication I was administered during surgery. My friend came in to check on me to see how I was doing. She said that the doctor stopped her in the hall and asked her a really strange question. I asked her what she meant by strange, and she said he wanted to know if I ever hallucinated. I asked her if she knew why the doctor was curious. The doctor told her that the anesthetist said when I was under that I talked about being aboard a flying saucer. I couldn't believe it. I asked her what else I had said, but she told me that was all the doctor mentioned. After all this time trying to get someone to administer Sodium Penathol, and all I said while I was under was that I was aboard a flying saucer. They checked me out of the hospital the same day under a lot of protest from me, because the pain had not yet subsided. Once home, I began to run a fever, so my friend phoned the doctor. He told her that he had accidentally cut one of my muscles, and when she asked him why he hadn't mentioned that to us, his only explanation was that he had forgotten. I immediately called the hospital and informed them of what had transpired. They told me if they had known that, I would certainly not have been released, but rather than have me check back in, they would have a prescription filled for the pain, and my friend could go back and pick it up. A few days later, when I felt better, I called the anesthetist's office to find out exactly what I had said, other than being aboard a flying saucer. He was in surgery when I called, so I left a message for him to return my call. I waited two days and still no reply from him. I phoned again and asked if he had been given my message, and the receptionist assured me that he had received it. I called repeatedly for two weeks, with no response from him. Finally, I asked my doctor to talk to him and to assure him that I would never mention his name, because all I wanted to know was what I said.

My doctor got back to me the next day and told me that I must have said something very strange, because the anesthetist didn't want to talk about it, and that he seemed to be scared. "Of what?" I asked. The doctor said that he wouldn't say, but that it seemed rather weird to him that whatever I had said had such an impact on the anesthetist. He said people babble things all the time under the effect of Sodium Penathol, such as even talking about murdering somebody, but nobody in the operating room pays any attention. I asked him if he thought there was any chance I could talk to the anesthetist myself, and he told me he didn't think so.

Chapter 40
Missing Hospital File

Approximately one year later, I called Dr. Harder. We started talking about my knee surgery, and I told him I was still very curious as to what I actually had said. He said he would talk to my doctor to see if he could get any new information for me, but I told him that I very much doubted he'd be able to get anywhere with him. Dr. Harder then suggested that I request a copy of my medical records, because he said they should contain a recording and possibly even a video of my surgery. I hadn't thought of the possibility of there being a video. I was elated, because maybe I could finally find out what I said while under the Sodium Penathol. I called my surgeon's office and asked his secretary for a copy of my files. I told her I was especially interested in what I said to the anesthetist, and she said she would talk to the doctor and call me back. When she returned my call, she informed me that, according to the files, I didn't have anesthesia. I assured her that I did, because, after all, they performed surgery on my knee, so I obviously had to have had anesthesia. She said she was sorry, but her records did not indicate that I had an anesthetist. She suggested that I contact the hospital and request a copy of their records. Next, I telephoned the hospital record's department, and I was informed that the hospital had recently filed bankruptcy, and that all the medical records were sent to Southern California. They gave me a telephone number for the facility in Southern California, so I phoned the facility and explained what I needed. He said he would request the file and call me when he received it from storage. The next day, he called back to tell me that my medical records were missing from their files. I asked him if he was sure, and he said he had double checked on it himself, and clearly, it was missing from their records. My file was listed on their record's index, but when he pulled the box from storage, my file was empty. He said he had no idea where my records might have gone, and that they had no record of pulling the file for anyone else. Apparently, it was just gone. I couldn't believe what I had just heard. I phoned Dr. Harder and told him what had happened. He agreed that it was very strange that my file would be missing, because he told me that when a facility goes into bankruptcy, all of the files have to be turned over. I asked him if he thought there was anything else I could do, and he didn't have a clue. I then called Dr. Harold and asked him what he thought about my missing file, and he said that he didn't know, but that he, too, found it to be very disturbing that someone had clearly taken my file.

Chapter 41
More Clues

I kept telling myself to just let all of this stuff go. I needed to get on with my life and try to forget that any of this had ever happened to me. Just when I thought maybe I could move on, I'd get another idea on how to track down another lead. I ran into Warren Hinkle at Hanno's one day, and we started talking about the Illuminati again. He told me to check with the FBI. "Oh, yeah, sure, I just call up the FBI and ask them to give me all the information they have?", I joked. He explained that I had a right to the information under the "Freedom of Information Act." The Act provides that most government agencies have to give you the information requested, and he instructed me on how to go about requesting the information. I decided that I had nothing to lose by giving it a try. I sent my letter off to the FBI, and, lo and behold, they did have a file on the Illuminati! I couldn't believe it. They had 48 pages but could only release 47 of them. After reviewing the 47 pages that they did send to me, I thought it was a little strange that they didn't release the 48th page, because almost every page that they sent me was redacted, and I wondered why they couldn't have redacted that particular page, as well. There was only one name in the file that wasn't blacked out, and it was the name of a doctor in Indiana. I decided to call information to see if they had a listing for him, and, much to my surprise, they did have a phone number for him. A woman answered the phone, and I asked for Dr. Hayes. She asked me for my name, and I decided not to give her my real name, so I told her I was John Holmes. She then asked me if Dr. Hayes knew me, and I told her that he did not, but that it was very important I speak with him. She put me on hold for, what seemed to be, an eternity, and then, finally, Dr. Hayes came on the line and asked me what he could do for me. I asked him if he could give me any information on the Illuminati. There was a long pause, and I was beginning to wonder if he had walked away from the phone, but then he guardedly asked me how I got his name. I told him that I had obtained the file from the FBI, and he wondered just how I managed to do that. I explained the "Freedom of Information Act" to him. He was obviously a little leery of me, so he started asking me a lot of questions about myself. He wanted to know where I lived. I told him San Francisco. He asked who our mayor was, and I replied Diane

Feinstein. Again, he asked me what my name was, and I once again told him John Holmes. I decided he was trying to track me down, so I ended the conversation and hung up. A few days later, I decided to call him back and tell him everything, and then maybe he would trust me enough to give me some information on the Illuminati. He did seem to relax a little after listening to my story. He told me that he had been under the impression that the Illuminati was out of business, but after the information I had given him, obviously they were not. Again, I asked him if he could give me any information on them, and he told me that the real authority on the Illuminati was a doctor in Illinois. He gave me his number and told me that he would call first and let the doctor know I would be contacting him. I thanked him for his time and hung up. I then called Warren and told him what I had come up with, and he told me to get Robert Anton Wilson's book about the Illuminati, and he also recommended that I watch the movie The Parallax View. I was delighted that I was able to find both the book and the movie. The movie was about subliminal programming. I remembered seeing the Cinema Educational Guild mentioned in the FBI file, and I wondered if this was part of the subliminal group, and that the Rosacrutions was the recruiting arm. Then I realized that even if all of this were true, who would listen to me, because I'm probably just another UFO nut, as far as everyone is concerned. I read Robert Anton Wilson's book, but it was just a parody, poking fun at anyone who took this conspiracy stuff seriously.

I retraced all of my trails since the beginning of my experience leading me to this point, when, all of a sudden, it struck me that all the last names of the people I worked with in this investigation began with the letter "H"----- Dr. Hart, Dr. Hatcher, Dr. Harold, Dr. Hayes, Warren Hinkle, Dr. Harder, Dr. Haines, Dr. Hynek and my real last name, which was Holmes. I was clueless as to what this might mean. Probably just more pieces to the giant jigsaw puzzle I was trying to put together, or maybe I was trying too hard to figure out something that I should just let go.

Chapter 42
CIA-FBI

I decided that I would see if I could get any information on the Illuminati from the CIA, since the file the FBI sent me was mostly blacked out. They wrote back to me explaining that they had received numerous inquiries about the Illuminati, but after a thorough investigation, they were unable to find any information.

Chapter 43
Television Appearance

I received a call from Channel Four asking me to appear on a show they were airing on UFOs. One of the guests was going to be Whitley Strieber, who had a book out called Communion. It was about UFO abduction. I was intrigued by Whitley's story, so I agreed to appear, with the hope that maybe we could exchange information. When I arrived at the station before the program, there were four people waiting to appear on the show, and they were all staring at me. Whitley was one of them, and the other three were with the Center for UFO Studies from Arizona. After the show, they invited me to join them for lunch. At the restaurant, I asked them why they were all staring at me so intently when I walked into the room at the station. They claimed that they saw an immediate recognition between Whitley and myself, as though we knew each other, and then they asked me to explain what I had experienced. When I mentioned Rah, they all looked at each other. I asked them what was wrong, and they told me that the two common denominators with abductees was that they had been abducted more than once, and that the name Rah had popped up. This was news to me. They showed me pictures taken from a satellite of Mars that depicted, what appeared to be, pyramids. It brought to mind what the Ouija Board had said, and also what Sylvia Brown had told me. Well, now I had some more information that I didn't know what to do with. After I returned home, I telephoned Dr. Harold and asked him if he had seen the pictures of Mars, and he indicated that he had. My next question was whether he thought there were pyramids on Mars, and he said he just didn't have enough information. He went on to say that we have a lot of natural formations here on earth that are similar, but that were created by natural elements, and not made
by man or by aliens.

Chapter 44
Weekly World News

The telephone was ringing as I was coming in the door after work one evening. I picked it up, and it was a reporter from the Weekly World News. He asked me if I was a wacko. I told him that I wasn't, but that obviously he was, and I hung up on him. The next week, I noticed on the bulletin board at work a headline "The Terror of Bigfoot", and I wondered what it was about. I went over to check it out more closely, and then I noticed an article next to it. I couldn't believe what I was reading. The article started out with "John Clark driven to the brink of insanity." In the background, some of my co-workers were saying "Here, Puffy", and they were whistling. I remembered one day when I walked up to a fellow worker whom I didn't know very well, and he immediately backed away from me. I had asked him what was wrong, and he said to get away from him, because he knew I was that UFO nut. I asked him if he would calm down and let me tell him what had happened. Grudgingly, he did listen, and at the end of my story, he looked me straight in the eye and said "Okay, you're not crazy." "Of course I'm not" I said, and I explained that I was a normal person, and that I couldn't control all of the strange things that happened to me. I knew it had been a mistake to ever have given my story to the media, but, at the time, I thought it might help me get some answers. Instead, it ended up causing me a tremendous amount of anguish. I couldn't help but wish that everyone would have a little more compassion. When I won the airplane, I encountered jealousy, then ridicule and finally fear. There was a rumor going around that my boss was afraid to reprimand me, because he was thought that I might have him vaporized. Give me a break! I thought people were a little more sophisticated in the 80's because of all the information available about UFO's, but obviously they were not. I ignored the shouting and whistling and just went about my work.

Chapter 45
Crash in Bakersfield

Dr. Harold invited me to join him on an investigation of a crash near Bakersfield. The crash site was in a farmer's field. As we drove up, we noticed the pasture was completely devastated. I asked Dr. Harold if the crash had actually caused all that damage, but he said he didn't think so. The farmer explained that he had been out in his field, when suddenly he saw an object coming in low over his trees. At first, he thought it was an airplane, but since it was nearly dusk, he wasn't able to see it clearly. When he realized that it was going to crash, he ran for his house and called the sheriff's department, and within minutes, people began to show up. He thought they were military at first, but then he noticed they didn't have any insignias. They immediately erected a tent over the crash site. Dr. Harold commented that they put up the tent to prevent satellites from picking it up. Next, they removed the object. The farmer went on to say that the strangest thing happened the following day. When we asked him what had happened, he said that they had dynamited his whole field, and they told him to keep his livestock away from the area. He said he asked them why, and they told him that there was too much radiation coming from the ground. The farmer asked them what exactly had crashed in his pasture, and he was told that it was a stealth fighter. On the trip home, I asked Dr. Harold why they would have dynamited the whole field. His theory was that by dynamiting the entire area, nobody would be able to ascertain the exact location of the crash site, nor would anyone be able to take any measurements. An article appeared in the newspaper the next day about a stealth fighter crashing in a farmer's field, but there were no follow-up articles.

Chapter 46
Southern California

I was packing for a trip to Southern California to visit my kids when the phone rang. It was Fred. I told him about my trip, and he urged me to go to the Psychic Institute in San Diego. "No more psychic institutes for me", I told him. Not one easy to give up, he went on to say that the institute in San Diego was doing a lot of research into kirihan photography. I asked him what he was talking about, and he explained that it was a method of photographing someone's aura. To get Fred off the phone, I told him I would drive down and check it out, but I actually had no intention of making the drive to San Diego. This was merely a trip to see my children.

I took the kids to Disneyland and Knott's Berry Farm, and we really had a great time. They were very excited about the fact that they had seen my picture in the Weekly World News. They asked me why the article said I had come in contact with Bigfoot, and I told them that I had no idea. I asked them if they had seen Ralph lately. They said Ralph and his wife had divorced, and he was living in Compton. They said their mother had his address, so when I dropped the kids off, I got it from her and drove over to Ralph's. I was anxious to talk to him, as it had been several years since I last saw him. When he opened the door, I barely recognized him, because he was terribly unkempt. He was unshaven and his clothes were filthy and wrinkled, which puzzled me, because I had always remembered Ralph as being very much the "Dapper Dan" type. I asked him what had happened to him and where he had been all these years. He invited me in, and I was appalled by all the dirty dishes in the sink and the general disarray of the place. He said that he and Olivia had moved to St. Louis shortly after our camping trip, and then their marriage became very rocky, and they were arguing all the time. I asked him what they were arguing about, and he explained that mostly they argued about his drinking. I was surprised about that, too, because Ralph had never been much of a drinker. He said that after our camping trip, he started having trouble sleeping and he had many nightmares. I asked him if he wanted to talk about what happened that night at the campground, because maybe it would help him put it to rest. I asked him to describe the thing he saw standing next to me, and he shocked me by saying that there was more than one. "What are you talking about? I only saw one!" He said that the other one went in another direction. I asked him what they were doing when he noticed them, and he said that they were placing me back on the picnic table, and then one of them saw him watching them. He said he would never forget those eyes. I asked him to describe the eyes, and he said they were like cats' eyes, yellow with black slits. My mind raced back to the hypnosis session with Dr. Hart, and my description of the eyes was exactly as Ralph had just described them. I asked him what happened next, and he said that was when he threw the frying pan, and I started to wake up. I asked him what they were wearing, and Ralph said that one of them was wearing what appeared to be a black or purple cloak. I asked him if he remembered anything else, but he said that was all he saw. He asked me then what I had been up to all of these years, and I told him about all the leads I had followed trying to get to the bottom of what we encountered in Sequoia. I asked him if anything unusual had happened to him since our camping trip, but I was both relieved and delighted when he said he was thankful that nothing had happened to him since that night. I could tell he was getting anxious for me to leave, so I told him that my wife and I also were divorced, and that if he ever needed any thing, to please call me. That was the last time I saw Ralph. My kids told me later that he moved again, but that they didn't know where. I hoped that he was all right.

Chapter 47
Ralph San Diego

I decided to call the Physic Institute in San Diego after all. I made an appointment for the following day. This time there were only three people in the room with me. After relating my story to them, they informed me that what I had encountered was a mammal that left Greenland before the Ice Age. Oh boy, their theory was even worse than that of the people at the San Francisco Institute. I wondered where they came up with this stuff, and I was out of there in a hurry.

Chapter 48
Rosarito Beach, Mexico

Since I was so close to the border, I decided to drive down to Rosarito Beach, because I had flown there years ago and always remembered it as a great place. I had fond memories of the Rosarito Beach Hotel, so that was my first stop. I took a seat at the bar. A guy sitting next to me introduced himself and told me that this was his first time visiting Rosarito, and that he was from Washington, D.C. I told him I was from San Francisco. I asked him what he did for a living, and he said he worked for the National Archives. I remembered the Coast Guard officer telling me that all the files were sent to the National Archives, so I asked him if he had seen any information that would lead him to believe that flying saucers did exist. He said he had read many interesting articles over the years that would lead him to believe that they do exist. When pressed, he wouldn't go into detail. I asked him if he had ever heard of the Illuminati. He briskly told me that he hadn't, and he left the bar. I wondered why he reacted so strongly to the Illuminati. I didn't see him again.

In the morning, I walked down the beach to the airplane runway. A couple of planes were parked, and I heard the sound of a plane circling overhead. I looked up and recognized it as a Piper. The pilot finally decided to land, and I noticed that he didn't make a very good landing. You don't make a three-point landing with tricycle gear and a crosswind, I thought to myself. The door opened, and a very attractive woman climbed out of the plane, and right behind her was a man in a black leather jumpsuit. I walked over and asked him if he needed a hand tying down. He appreciated my offer, and afterwards he offered to buy me a drink. I told him that it was a little too early for cocktails, but that he could buy me a cup of coffee, so we headed for the restaurant. I told him that I, too, was a pilot. He introduced himself as Bob and said that he was a Hollywood producer. I asked him what he had produced, and he said he had mostly done television specials, one of them being on Mama Cass of the Mama's and the Papa's. We ended up really hitting it off and made arrangements to meet the next day at Van Nuys Airport to fly over to Catalina Island.

Chapter 49
Catalina Island

I phoned my boss and made arrangements to extend my trip for a few days. I called my old boss, Herb, to tell him of my plans, and he invited me to stay with him for a few days. Next, I called the Van Nuys airport and asked if they had a plane available for the next day. They reserved one for me and told me to be there an hour before takeoff for a checkout flight. As I was going through the check ride, I heard Bob call the tower for landing instructions. My check ride went fine, although it had been awhile since I had flown in the Los Angeles basin. I hadn't thought then that it could get anymore crowded, but it certainly had, as there were a lot of aircraft up there. Downwind leg, there were twelve aircraft trying to land. It was truly amazing to me that there weren't more midair collisions. We taxied back to the FBO, and I went inside to get a soda. I noticed that Bob was taxing up to get gas, so I walked out to greet him. Once he was gassed up, we decided that I would lead the way, so I took off first, but Bob was right behind me. "Nice take off" I heard him say. "Thanks" I replied. Once we cleared airport control, I told Bob to change frequencies. I told him we'd go midfield LAX, then when we hit the coastline, we'd climb to 3500 ft. It was a CAVU (clean air visibility unlimited) day. "Hey Bob, did you see that beautiful Skymaster that just went by?" "Sure did" he replied. When we reached the coastline, I started to climb. There was a regulation that any time you flew over water, you had to have floatation gear or be at an altitude high enough that if your engine quit you would be able to glide to land. "Hey Bob, did that Citation just pass you?" "What Citation?" he asked. "The one that just passed me." "No" was his reply. I banked my plane to see where Bob was, and I noticed that he was not behind me. I banked starboard, and there he was heading off in another direction following another aircraft. Just then, I heard that sound again----"Oh no!" I gasped. My engine was quitting. I started my emergency checklist. Fuel was on a proper tank, mags turned on fuel pump, set up best glide ratio, . . . then my mind flashed back to Hawaii. Here I am, once again, going down over a channel of water. I wondered what was going on. I had to make a decision fast, to make either a 180 or try to make it to Catalina, or, the very last thing that I wanted to do -- make a water landing. A water landing in this plane would not be a good idea, since it did not have retractable gear. The odds were that when I hit the water, I would cartwheel. Boy, what great choices, I thought to myself. The airport at Catalina was on the top of a mountain on a 1,000 ft. table top field. I began to apply carburetor heat, and I decided to try and make it to Catalina. I told myself that at least this aircraft didn't have the sink rate that the twin had in Hawaii. I thought that if I had to, I could try and make a beach landing. I noticed I was now down to 800 ft., so the airport landing was definitely out of the question. I was searching for any beach that I could set down on, and it wasn't looking too promising. "Catalina Unicom, I have a problem." "Who's calling?" I was so busy that I had neglected to give my aircraft number. "Catalina Unicom Cherokee 2438 Alpha Romeo. It looks like I am going to have to make a water landing. Have no Engine" "What is your position?" "Cherokee 2438 Alpha Romeo. Approximately 3 miles NE Avalon" was my reply. "All right, we will notify the Coast Guard. Good luck." My knees were shaking so badly on the rudder, that I had to reach down and try to hold them steady. I was still attempting to restart the engine. Then, at 200 ft., I heard the sound of the engine starting. "Come on baby, fire!" Sure enough the engine started. I pulled back on the yoke and as I started to climb, I could have sworn that I saw a shark fin sticking out of the water. "Catalina Unicom, Cherokee 2438 Alpha Romeo." "Go ahead Cherokee 2438." "Yeah, it looks like I have power back. Will land at airport." Next, I heard Catalina advising traffic that they had an emergency and to clear approach for me. I have never been so glad to land. I taxied over to the tie down and was directed to the office to fill out a report. I gave the person Bob's number and asked him to let Bob know where I was when he landed. I then headed into the office to complete my form. One of the questions on the form asked what was the cause of the engine failure. I wanted to keep my license so "unknown force" was out of the question. I answered that I suspected carburetor ice. After completing the paperwork, I went outside to check on Bob's status, and he was just landing. I realized then that my emergency landing must have caused a stack-up. I knew that I needed a drink. My hands were still shaking from my near crash landing. Once Bob was tied down, I asked him where he had gone, and he told me that somehow he had gotten off track and found himself behind another aircraft. When he heard me call Catalina Unicom, he knew he was following the wrong plane. He asked me what happened to my plane, and I told him that I didn't know. I asked him if he would mind spending the night in Catalina. Bob had a job to get back to, but he felt sure that I would be able to get a room down in Avalon. I explained that I really felt that I needed to unwind, and that if I had a drink, I wouldn't be able to fly back. He understood and gave me some recommendations on hotels to check with to see if I could get a room for the night. Once I had my lodgings taken care of, we had lunch together, and then he headed back. I checked into my room and stayed there for the rest of the night. I was wondering what in the world was going to happen next. Did these kinds of things happen to everyone, or was I being singled out? Once again, my nerves were becoming frayed, and I sure didn't want to end up back in the hospital. When I got up in the morning, I walked around Avalon. I had never been there before and was taken in by its charm and beauty. No wonder all the movie stars spend time in Avalon, I thought to myself. After walking around the village for a while, I decided that there was no putting off the inevitable. It was time to fly back. As I was going through my run-up, I was filled with trepidation and my knees began to shake uncontrollably. I kept telling myself over and over again that it would be all right. As I started to roll, I remembered that a lot of pilots had been killed at Catalina, because there was a hump in the runway making it look like you had reached the end of it, so the pilots would try to lift off. Then they would stall and go over the end of the runway. I had flown in and out of the Catalina airport many times, and it had never bothered me before, but now I was frightened beyond belief. As I took off, I flew over Avalon and headed toward the coastline. I couldn't shake the jitters through the entire flight back to Torrance, and I breathed a big sigh of relief when I finally touched down. When I was turning in the keys to the plane, the chief pilot asked me what had happened the day before. I told him the same thing that I wrote on the form - carburetor ice. He told me that he was glad I made it back all right, and I told him I was certainly glad that I did, too. It was time now for me to get back home.

Chapter 50
Aura Reading

The light on my answering machine was blinking furiously when I returned home from Southern California. Dr. Hatcher, Dr. Harold, Fred, Dr. Hart and Warren Hinkle had all left messages for me to contact them. I called Dr. Hatcher first and told him what happened. He scheduled an appointment for me for the following Wednesday. Next, I called Fred. Once again, Fred had someone he wanted me to meet. This time it was an expert on auras. I told Fred that I was growing weary of all these so-called "professionals" he insisted upon setting me up with. He promised me that this would be the last person he would send me to, and, of course, he had already set up an appointment for me to go the next day.

The "aura reader" had set up shop in an old building in the Haight. When I walked into his office, I was overwhelmed with the scent of incense. I hadn't smelled that since the sixties. Then a very tall bearded man appeared in the doorway. Fitting right in with his surroundings, he looked like someone from the sixties. "Wow, man, come on in." he said, and I was wondering what Fred had gotten me into this time. After a few preliminary questions, he introduced himself as Phil and filled me in on his " credentials." He claimed that he had not seen a blue green aura as intensely bright as mine. I asked him what he thought it meant, and he informed me that it meant I was blessed, and that somewhere in time I was a conqueror. He claimed that I also had something to do with the building of the pyramids. I thought it was interesting that this information tied into everything I had heard in the past from the Quiji Board and various psychics. I was wondering if everyone was on to something, or if maybe they just told this same thing to everybody. I thanked Phil for his time and made a hasty retreat. Driving home, I recalled a friend of mine telling me about a dream where the whole world was meeting at the Los Angeles Colosseum to plan what they were going to do to him the next day. I remembered thinking that my friend had completely lost it, and I was beginning to think that maybe I was losing it, too.

94

Chapter 51
The Search Goes on

A few days later, I called Warren Hinkle. I always thought of him as an objective bystander, so I asked him if he really thought I was taken aboard a flying saucer. There was a long pause after I asked him that leading question, but finally, he replied "Yes, I do." I asked him what, exactly, had made him come to that conclusion, when he had repeatedly told me that he didn't believe the Betty and Barney Hill story or Travis Walton's either. He explained that he felt that something out of the ordinary definitely had happened to me. He went on to say that he had been in the newspaper business for a long time, and that he was able to tell when someone was telling the truth, and he believed every word I told him. I asked him if he thought I would ever find out the real reason for everything that had been happening to me these past few years. He said that he didn't know, and then he commented that it may be for the best if I never find out the answers to my questions, because those answers may be difficult for me to live with.

Chapter 52
Pilot Citing

I decided to drive up to the airport where the plane I had won in Tahoe was tied down. I had sold the plane shortly after I won it, and I found myself driving up to the airport to look at it periodically, as if to remind myself that it really had happened. I had, indeed, won an airplane, and it wasn't all a dream. I went into the pilot's lounge and recognized Roger, the pilot instructor who had helped me check out the plane when I first received it. He remembered me and asked how I was doing, and if I was planning on flying that day. I explained that I was just there to check out my old plane. He mentioned that he had read the article about the UFO abduction, and we talked a bit about it. I felt as though Roger was fishing for some information from me, and my assumption was correct, because then he asked if he could share an experience that had recently happened to him. "Of course" I replied. He seemed somewhat embarrassed, and he said that he hadn't told anyone else what he was about to tell me, because he was afraid of losing his pilot's license. He said he hoped I would understand and hear him out. Roger said that one day he was at 8,000 feet over Lake Berryessa, when, out of nowhere, an orange light appeared. He called center and asked them how far his traffic was, and they said there was no traffic. He turned out his NAV. Lights, thinking that maybe they were reflecting off of the clouds. However, the orange light was still there. He then banked the plane, and he could see the reflection of the light on the wing of the plane. He then realized that it was a solid object. The orange object suddenly accelerated at an incredible speed, made a right angle turn and shot straight up through the clouds. Roger heard a pilot of a commercial jet on top of the clouds yell "What the hell was that?" There was a long silence on the radio, and then center asked both of them if they wanted to file a pilot report. Roger and the commercial pilot both declined. I asked Roger to describe what it looked like. He went over to the blackboard and drew what he had seen. The drawing looked like an egg with a ring spinning around it. I asked Roger if he objected to me telling someone about what he saw, and he was adamant that I not mention it to anyone. He explained that he only related the story to me because of my experience. I told him that I understood, and that the only person I wanted to relay the story to was a UFO investigator, and that he would be very discreet. He asked me the name of this investigator, and I told him Dr. Richard Harold. I encouraged him to check him out, if that would make him feel more at ease. After some consideration, Roger told me it would be okay for me to talk to Dr. Harold, but he requested that I not reveal his name. I assured him that I would not mention his name or in any way jeopardize his job. As soon as I returned home, I contacted Dr. Harold and told him about Roger's experience. He told me that Dr. Hynek was coming to town, and that he would be very interested in this, as Dr. Hynek was the consultant in astronomy for the Air force's so-called study of UFOs. After the Air force closed the project, Dr. Hynek continued his investigation, as he had said there were too many unanswered questions. I remembered calling Dr. Hynek after Dr. Hart told me that I had been abducted, and I had asked him his opinion of Dr. Hart. He had said that Dr. Hart was a very bright scientist, but sometimes he jumped to conclusions. I told Dr. Hynek that Dr. Hart was 99 percent sure that I had been abducted. Dr. Hynek replied that if Dr. Hart was that certain, I probably had been abducted, but, the question was, who or what did the abducting. When Dr. Hynek arrived in San Francisco, Dr. Harold called me and asked if I wanted to go with them to the airport to talk to Roger. I explained that I wouldn't be able to accompany them, because I had an appointment with Dr. Hatcher. I really wanted to meet Dr. Hynek, however, and I asked Dr. Harold if it would be at all possible for us to meet sometime later in the day. He said he didn't know what Dr. Hynek's schedule was like, but that he would check with him and leave a message for me on my answering machine if they could work something out.

Chapter 53
Dr. Hatcher

"So Dr. Hatcher, have you come to any conclusion as to what has been happening to me?" I asked. "No, John, I still don't know what we are dealing with in your case", he replied. I asked him what he thought of the idea of my giving up my search for answers to see if it would put an end to all the strange things that were happening to me. He thought about it for a minute and finally stated that he honestly didn't know. I asked him if he had ever encountered a case similar to mine, and, after giving it some thought, he replied that there had been one similar case several years ago. "What was the outcome?" I queried. "She died." My heart sank to my knees. My mind began to race---- would death be my fate, too? I asked him if he was ever able to ascertain what she had been dealing with, and he said that he had not. I realized then that it was a very distinct possibility that I would never be able to get the answers to all of my questions. "Chris, I'm going to stop my search". He looked very disappointed and said that he felt I might be really close to learning the truth. I told him that I wasn't entirely sure anymore if I could even handle the truth. I ended our session and told Dr. Hatcher that I would contact him if I decided to take up the chase again, but, for now, I was going fishing, literally. I just needed a break from everything and everyone. I was feeling a little sad saying goodbye to Chris for perhaps the last time, because we had been through a lot together, and even though I had my apprehensions, because of his involvement with the CIA, it had been comforting to talk with him. As I closed the door behind me, I saw the look of concern on Dr. Hatcher's's face.

Chapter 54
Life Returns to Normal

A few weeks later, while having lunch in a restaurant, I struck up a conversation with a woman sitting next to me and ended up telling her about my ordeal. She seemed fascinated by everything I told her and had so many questions. Our conversation was cut short, because she had to go, but she gave me her phone number and asked me to call her sometime. I phoned her a few days later, and when she answered, I asked her if she remembered me. She said "Oh yes, the alien astronaut." We both laughed, and I thought to myself that she seemed to have a great sense of humor, which was something I very much appreciated in a person. We began dating, and eventually she asked me to move in with her, her reasons being that she had a very large home, and her children were at the age where they would be graduating soon and leaving home, and, besides that, she was lonely. I agreed to her idea, and, as time went by, everything seemed to be working out well. All of the strange occurrences stopped happening, and it felt as though I had made the right decision. For the first time in years, everything in my life was going great. We spent almost every weekend up at the lake, and I was able to do a lot of fishing. One time, I came back into the camp with three large mouth bass, each of them weighing at least 5 pounds. One of the old timers at the camp couldn't believe that I'd actually caught the bass, and he said he was going to drive around the lake and find the fish truck that I had bought them from. I laughed and told him "Lots of luck." Yes, I thought to myself, I finally feel at peace.

When Beth and I had been together about a year and a half, we were on our way home from the lake one weekend, when she complained of having a severe headache. I told her it was probably allergies, and that once we were back home, she'd be fine. Unfortunately, this was not the case. The headaches persisted, and she began having problems with the vision in her right eye. She made an appointment with her doctor, and he recommended that she see a neu-rologist. She set up the appointment and after a battery of tests, he recommended that she see a particular brain surgeon at UCSF, who was considered one of the tops in his field. "A brain surgeon?", I exclaimed. "Yes" the doctor replied "she has a brain tumor." Oh no, I thought, it's starting to happen all over again. I remembered Bill, and I was having trouble getting control of myself. Beth made the appointment with the surgeon, and I accompanied her. After reviewing the catscan, the doctor explained that he had no option other than to operate. He showed me the pictures and explained that the tumor was on her optic nerve, and he said it was very rare to have a growth in that partic- ular location. He scheduled the date for her surgery, and we went home. Beth really handled the situation quite well, but I was a nervous wreck in the days prior to the surgery. When the day finally arrived, I paced the halls of the hos- pital for seven hours. Bill's death kept popping into my head, but I kept trying to override those negative thoughts by telling myself that Beth would come out of this okay. Finally, I saw the doctor coming down the hall in my direction. My heart was beating a mile a minute, but I kept telling myself to stay calm. After all, it had been nearly two years since anything out of the ordinary had happened. Everything has been going great, and this was just a bump in the road. Beth would be all right. "How is she?" I asked. "Damndest thing I have ever seen. I got in there, and the tumor just popped up. I've never seen any- thing like it." He kept shaking his head and repeating himself. I had to shake him to get his attention. "How's Beth?" I asked him again. He looked at me and shook his head "I'm terribly sorry, John, but she didn't make it." My mind went totally blank, and I was having a very difficult time breathing. I ran out of the hospital, and I kept asking myself why, why, why did this happen? I couldn't go on anymore. Who else was going to die because of me? I jumped in my car and just drove. I was driving down Highway 1, and my mind was telling me to just drive off one of the cliffs, but my body wouldn't respond. I ended up in Half Moon Bay. I parked the car and went into the Moonraker. I told the bartender to give me the strongest thing he had, which turned out to be 151 rum. I shot it back before he set the bottle down and told him to give me another. He looked at me and asked me if I was all right. "Other than the fact that my girlfriend just died in surgery, I'm fine. Now, are you going to give me another or what?" I angrily responded. "Just take it easy. This isn't light weight stuff you're slamming back." he said. I told him I needed the strong stuff in order to deal with the fact that I kept killing people who were close to me, not thinking how that must have sounded, but he continued to fill the glass every time I asked. Suddenly, there were bright lights above me, and I yelled "Turn off the lights!" Then I realized that I was on a gurney in an emergency room. I asked one of the nurses what I was doing in emergency, and she said that I had a nasty bump on the head. She said that when the police brought me in, they told the attendant that I had fallen off a barstool. I didn't remember a thing, but I had one hell of a headache. Perhaps that fall

100

was God's way of putting me out of my misery, for at least a little while.

Chapter 55
Escape

I moved up to the lake and stayed there for over a year. I became somewhat of a hermit, spending my days fishing and writing in my journal. Writing did seem to help me get over the loss of Beth. Looking at my experiences on paper was therapeutic. It was as if I were reading about someone else's life, instead of my own. That year at the lake really helped me get my head back on straight, and I probably would have stayed forever, but the 150 miles a day round-trip commute to work was beginning to wear me out. I eventually moved back closer to "civilization."

Chapter 56
New Business Opportunity

After I moved away from the lake, it didn't take long to get back into a regular routine, and I contacted some friends that I hadn't seen in the past year. One of my buddies, Mike, told me that he had been trying to find me, because he had something interesting to discuss with me. He was very excited about a new product that a friend of his had invented. Mike knew my background in sales and marketing, and he was anxious for me to get together with his friend. I told him to arrange a time and I would be there. The following week, I met Mike and his friend, Ed, at a restaurant where Ed was a waiter. Ed showed me the product, and it was truly amazing. If you lost a cork in a wine bottle, this gadget went down and pulled it out. I told Ed that I thought it was great, so he asked me if I would take a ride up to the wine country with him to talk to someone about financing. I told him I'd be happy to go along. Our destination was Valley of the Moon Winery. The owner was interested in putting up money for the cork retriever. He told Ed that he would put up $10,000 to get it off the ground, and Ed was ecstatic. On the way back, he told me that he would like to have me on board. I asked him in what capacity, and he said he wanted me to be the marketing sales director. I was wondering to myself if this was something I'd be able to handle, but I decided that I needed to give it a try. After all, it was a great product, and it could be a lot of fun, as well as quite a challenge, to try to put together a successful marketing plan. I told Ed that I was definitely ready to give it a shot. We began working on the design, and I came up with the name and slogan. It would be called Wine Waiter, and the slogan would be "Don't Blow Your Cork!" We decided to debut the Wine Waiter at the Gourmet Food and Wine Show in San Francisco at Moscone Center. We really had to get going with the development of the prototype and packaging, since the show was less than six months away. We were able to get it ready in time for the show, and I lined up some friends of mine to help out. Our booth was decorated with balloons, and we managed to generate a lot of excitement and became the hit of the show. I was walking around the exhibition, when I saw Danny Kaye standing at one of the booths. I went over, tapped him on the shoulder and asked him if I could show him something. He asked me if it was a new product, and, when I told him that it was, he whistled for his entourage, and they all followed me to our booth. He really liked the Wine Waiter, so I told him he could keep the demonstrator he had just used. When Ed came back to the booth, I told him what had happened. Much to my surprise, he was furious that I had given one of the products away. I was totally shocked by his response, and I then realized that he had absolutely no concept of what it takes to market a product. This was the first indication that there would be trouble down the road. Several minutes later, I noticed that a lot of people were gathering around the booth. They were reporters and said they wanted to take pictures of our product. It turned out that Danny Kaye had sent them over to take the photos, so that they could feature it on their show. He had also told them that he felt that it was a terrific product and was going to show the Wine Waiter that I gave him to everyone he knew. "You just got a million dollars worth of free publicity!" one reporter said. People were asking me what I was going to do with my first million. I couldn't believe it. This must be a dream. Things were definitely looking up! The following night I received a phone call from one of the demonstrators. She wanted to know if she could be involved with the company, so I told her that she would have to check with Ed. Little did I know that this was the beginning of the end for the Wine Waiter. I received a phone call from Ed the next day, and he asked if I could meet him for lunch. I knew that something was wrong. He explained that he had someone who wanted to invest $50,000 in the company, and I told him that was great. But he said that there was one catch, which was that the investors wanted to be in charge of marketing and sales. "Wait a minute, that's my position!", I exclaimed. "What's the difference, John? You're still a shareholder?" I told him that I realized that I was still a shareholder, but marketing this product was my baby, and I didn't think that anybody could market it as well as I could. I asked him who the investors were, and he said it was Cindy and her boyfriend. She was the demonstrator at the show, and the one who had called me about getting on board. She knew the company needed money, and she got her boyfriend to put up the $50,000. She basically bought my job. Ed told me that he still wanted me to handle the demonstrations at the department stores and specialty shops, which I agreed to do. Cindy and her boyfriend tried to copy everything I did, but they didn't have a clue about marketing. They ended up driving the company into the ground. One day I went over to the office to confront them about a problem with the inventory at one of the major department stores. I told Ed that we needed to have a company meeting, and he said he would set one up for the next day. As I was leaving, I noticed a pendant around Cindy's neck. I knew I had seen it somewhere before, but I couldn't remember where. I glanced at it again, trying to jog my memory. On the way home, I was sitting in traffic, and it came to me where I had seen that pendant before. The woman at the Rosacrution's headquarters had been wearing the same pendant. Chills ran up and down my spine---was there a correlation here, or was this just a coincidence? It wasn't very long before the company was ruined. It turned out that the money Cindy's boyfriend put into the company was really just a short term loan, and they were taking the money out of what was coming in. I told Ed that I wanted out and sold half of my shares. I kept the other half as a souvenir.

Chapter 57
Cosmic Clearance

One day I received a telephone call from an unidentified caller. He asked me if I knew anything about cosmic clearance. I said that I did not. I asked who was calling and the caller responded "just a friend." Right away, I thought of Tom Jolie. I couldn't imagine, after all these years, that they were back. However, I decided to play along. "Okay, tell me, what is cosmic clearance?" I asked. "It's clearance above top secret" the caller answered. "How do you know this?" I asked. "Because I have the clearance" was the caller's response. "So, why are you calling me?" I queried. "Because I can give you information that will help you" the caller replied. I asked the caller what kind of information, and he responded by telling me he had information on aliens and the Illuminati. This certainly got my attention, so I asked him to explain. He put me off and said that he couldn't talk about it over the phone and would prefer to meet with me in person. I expressed some reservations about agreeing to a meeting, but he then told me to look in my mailbox, because I would find a package there. He told me to review the material in the package and after doing so, to call this number: 202-555-1234. Then the caller hung up. I decided to go down and see if there really was anything in the mailbox. I must say that I was surprised when I opened it and found that there actually was a package inside. I reached in and carefully took it out. I went back upstairs and put it on the living room table. My hands were trembling as I attempted to open it, because the thought crossed my mind that it could be a bomb. I stopped for a minute just to take a quick look outside to see if anyone was lurking around. I didn't see anyone, and my curiosity was getting the best of me, so I decided to go back inside and open the package. It was quite a lengthy procedure, because I took such care not to bump or move the box as I, ever so gently, cut the tape. When I finally got the package opened, I glanced at the clock on the wall and was startled to see that it had been over an hour since I received the anonymous phone call. The top document in the package was my letter that I had sent to the FBI asking about the Illuminati. Underneath that, was the letter I sent to the CIA regarding the same subject. I was wondering how he was able to obtain copies of these letters, and then I noticed he had included all of the newspaper articles about me winning the airplane and about the UFO over the casino. There was a copy of Warren's story., and a picture of my car after it had been destroyed by fire. There were other pictures that had me completely baffled, because I didn't have a clue as to how they were taken. He had even included taped conversations that I had with many of the people that I worked with. There was a report on the Illuminati describing who they were, and how they had infiltrated all of the governments in the world. After looking over all the material, I called the operator and asked her if she could tell me what part of the country had the area code 202. When she told me Washington, D.C., I just hung up the phone. I didn't know what to think. I decided to call the number he had given me and find out how he had obtained all of the material. I heard "Be at home at 6:00 p.m. EDT for telephonic contact." It sounded to me like some kind of answering machine recording, but it didn't allow me to leave a message. Instead, it merely disconnected me. When the phone rang, I nearly jumped out of my skin. "Hello, Mr. Clark. Was that enough to convince you?", the caller asked. "How did you get all of those items? What's your name?" I asked. "Just call me Bob for now.", he replied. He went on to tell me that many ET groups are operating on this planet and some of them are not very nice. When I asked him what he meant by that, he informed me that they play games up to and including killing people. He said that his people felt that I had contact with such a group, and that they wanted to meet with me in Washington, D.C. They felt that I might be able to help put an end to the dangerous ET groups. My mind was racing a mile a minute. What did they want with me? Who exactly are these people? How did they obtain all of that personal information on me? When will this ever end? I wish that I could just walk away from all of this, which is what I thought I had done. I told Bob that I wouldn't be able to make the trip to Washington, D.C., but that I wanted to have some time to think it over. I asked him for a telephone number, and he told me to use the number he had given me earlier. Before he hung up, he told me he hoped that he would hear from me soon, because time was running out. I asked him what he meant by that, and he said I would understand when I met with his people in Washington. With that remark he hung up.

I remembered having a conversation with Dr. Hart about the various alien groups that he knew of, and I decided to give him a call to see if I could get any new information from him. He told me that he had found out that many more alien groups existed than he had originally thought. I asked him if they were involved with the government, and he said that he believed that some were involved. I asked him how many groups he thought existed, and he said that he believed that there were close to a 100 groups. I asked him then if he felt that the country was in any danger, and he said that it could be if the wrong ETs gain control. I thanked him for the information and hung up. I wondered if perhaps Dr. Hart and "Bob" were connected, and if they were, why were they dragging me into all of this.

Chapter 58
Motorcycle Accident

I decided to take a ride on my motorcycle to try to clear my mind. I rode out to the coast, and afterwards, headed into the city. I decided to go to Chinatown to get something to eat. I was stopped at a light, waiting for it to turn green. When it finally did, I entered the intersection and saw something coming at me out of the corner of my eye. Before I could react, I was hit by a truck that had come right through the red light, and I went sailing off the motorcycle. I must have been unconscious for a minute or two. When I realized what had happened, I tried to get up to get to my motorcycle, so that I could turn off the engine, but I was unable to do so. It felt as though my leg was broken. I ended up crawling over to my bike and did manage to get the engine turned off. I was afraid to look at my leg, because I thought I might see a bone sticking out of it. Another motorcyclist came by and asked if he could help. I asked him to take care of my bike, so he picked it up and got it off the street. An ambulance showed up next, and they put a neck brace on me and put my leg in a splint. They loaded me into the ambulance, and, as we were on the way to the hospital, one of the medics asked me why I was riding in Chinatown. "Why not?" I asked. "You know the slogan of China Airlines don't you?" I said that I did not. "You've seen our driving, now watch our flying" was his response. A real jokester I thought to myself. I guess they were trying to get my mind off of the pain in my leg, but their method didn't work. In the emergency room, they started to cut my brand new jeans off, and, even though I protested vehemently, it was no use. They took x-rays, and, fortunately, my leg was not broken. My parents were nice enough to come down to the hospital to pick me up. During my recovery period, I kept wondering if my accident had anything to do with the phone call from "Bob." I didn't attempt to contact him again and hoped that if I didn't call him, he wouldn't call me.

Chapter 59
Pleasant Close Encounter

A few months after the accident, I decided I was in good enough shape to take the bike out again. I rode up the coast of Marin County and came back down Highway 101. I spotted a Mexican restaurant on the side of the freeway and stopped in to get something to eat. As I walked in, I noticed two ladies sitting at the bar. I couldn't help but notice how pretty one of them was. I decided to go over and introduce myself, and up close, I saw that she really was beautiful. She seemed to have a great sense of humor, and we talked all afternoon. I asked her for a date, and she said she would like that. We kept going out, and I couldn't believe how lucky I was, once again, to find such a nice person. After a period of time, we moved in together, and it was like heaven. Everything was working out well. We had a lot of fun together, as she enjoyed riding the motorcycle nearly as much as I did, and we rode it together very often. We both enjoyed traveling and went to a variety of places. She mentioned one time that she had never been to Washington, D.C. I told her that I had spent a lot of time there, and I would love to go back sometime, so we made that our next vacation destination. In the back of my mind, I was thinking that I could contact that Bob character to see if I could find out what was going on.

Chapter 60
Washington, D.C.

We made the necessary plans for our trip. I called the number Bob had given me and left a message as to when I'd be in the area. We flew into Washington National at night, and I pointed out some of my favorite points of interest to her. She was very excited, and I was looking forward to showing her everything. I told her that I would meet her at the baggage claim area, because I needed to use the men's room. While I was in the restroom, the man next to me said, "Mr. Clark?" Without even thinking about it, I said "Yes?" He told me to be at the Washington Monument the next day at 3:00 p.m., and then he walked out. As you can probably imagine, I was dumbstruck and beginning to wonder if I should have made that call to Bob after all. When I met up with my girlfriend at the baggage claim, she asked me if anything was wrong. I guess I must have looked a little shaken. I assured her that everything was fine, and we gathered our bags and headed for the hotel.

The next morning we went out to Mount Vernon and then on to Arlington Cemetery. I asked her where she would like to go next, and she said the National Art Gallery. I asked her if it would be all right with her if I dropped her off there, since I wasn't really into art. I explained that I would like to spend some time in the Air & Space Museum right across the street, and we could meet at the restaurant in the Art Gallery around 5:00. She thought that was a great idea, and I was relieved, because that would give me enough time to get to the Washington Monument and back, without her realizing I was gone. I knew that if I were truthful and told her about my appointment, she would be terribly worried.

I arrived at the monument 30 minutes early. I was reminiscing about how I used to walk up the stairs to the top of the monument and run back down. I noticed that there were a lot of people milling around, and I was checking out the crowd, when someone from behind tapped me on the shoulder. I turned around, and I couldn't believe my eyes. It was Tom Jolie!

Tom explained that he had someone else make the telephone call to make sure that I would show up. He told me that he figured I wouldn't agree to the meeting if I knew it was him. I asked him why he asked me to come all the way to Washington to meet with him, and he said that they were having a problem. I asked him who "they" were and who exactly was he working with? I also told him that Dr. Hart had warned me that he was with military intelligence (now that's an oxymoron). Tom cut me off and told me that he couldn't give me much information, and the bottom line was that they wanted to "help" me. I asked him what it was, exactly, that they were planning to help me with. Tom said that I had information that his people could use, information that the aliens gave me. I was stunned. I couldn't believe what I was hearing. He went on to say that they knew about aliens for quite some time, and that, in fact, they were working with them until things got a little out of control. I asked what he meant by that, and he asked me if I had ever heard about the crash in Roswell, New Mexico. I told him that I had, of course, heard about the Roswell incident. Apparently, there were others that had crashed before in remote regions of the country and around the world, and Tom's people were able to recover some of them intact, as well as some of the occupants. Wait a minute! What was he saying? His people have live aliens in captivity? According to Tom, my encounter was with the group that had placed an implant in me when I was very young. My mind then flashed back to the Santa Cruz Mountains. This was getting crazier by the minute! Tom asked me if I remembered Dr. Hart telling Fred that he thought I was one of "them." I, indeed, remembered Dr. Hart's comment. Tom's opinion was that Dr. Hart was partially correct, but that I was used as a monitor. I asked him how he came to this conclusion. "They have done it to many humans." He went on to explain that the only reason I knew anything about what happened to me on the camping trip was because Ralph saw them returning me. Okay, okay, I thought, but what about all of the other strange occurrences? "Did they have anything to do with me winning the airplane?" He said yes. "Why?", I asked, but there was no response from Tom. This planet is an experiment, and the most effective way to monitor its progress is to place sensors in humans. I remembered the Ouija board saying that this planet was an experiment to see if we could all live together in peace. I asked Tom to tell me more about his work with them. We have been working with the aliens, allowing them to keep abducting humans in exchange for technology. He said that the reason technology has advanced so quickly in the past fifty years is because of the exchange of information with the aliens. The stealth plane was from alien technology, as were many other things, like the microwave and lasers, and he went on to name many things that I never would have thought about. "Then the government discovered that some of the aliens were cloning humans with their DNA, so that they could exist in

112

this environment. It wasn't long before things started to get out of control. Now, it's to the point that they don't know who's who. That's why they contacted me, and apparently others like me, to help. They figured that since I have an implant in me, I might be able to help detect the clones." I started laughing and said "Okay, Tom, the joke is over. This is too far over the top even for me!". He looked at me and then asked me if I really believed that all of the things that had happened to me over the years were just a joke. As I thought about it, the years of terror and anguish were definitely not funny. If what Tom was saying was true though, he really could have helped me, but he didn't. Why should I believe him now?

Before I could make any sense of anything he had just told me, he asked me to go for a ride with him. He assured me that it was close by and wouldn't take long. I knew it was getting close to the time I was to meet my girlfriend, but my curiosity was getting the best of me. As we were riding along in the car, I asked him if he had any idea if any members of government had been cloned. He said that he would put me in touch with people that they knew definitely had not been cloned, once I agreed to help. I began to wonder just what I had gotten myself into this time. After all, everything had calmed down recently. Maybe I should just let this go, once and for all. Then the car pulled up to an unmarked, gated drive. Tom told the guard that he was taking a visitor inside, and we were waved on through the gate. The roadway led to a very large building, and as we approached it, a garage door opened, and Tom drove inside. We walked down a long, tiled hallway that had nothing on the walls. It was a very sterile atmosphere, reminding me of a hospital. When we came to an elevator, we stepped inside, and Tom punched a button. The elevator descended for several minutes, making me wonder just how far underground we had actually traveled. The doors opened, and we walked down another long corridor, until it ended at a wall of stainless steel doors. Tom inserted an identification card into an electronic device, which I had only seen done in the movies, and it made me wonder what I was getting myself into. The doors opened, and as we passed through them, I felt as though I were stepping into a freezer, because the temperature was 30 to 40 degrees. Tom turned on the lights, and there, in front of us, were about 20 tables covered with white sheets. We walked by a few of them, before Tom stopped in front of one and asked me to take a look. He pulled back the sheet, and at first it didn't register with me what I was actually seeing. Tom was staring at me waiting for my reaction. "Oh my God! No!"

THE END

Additional Services & Resources of Information

Bar Code Graphics, Inc. - Call (800) 662-0701

Copyright Registration Service – ($40 Application Preparation) x144

Gold Foil Autograph Copy Labels – (Set of 100 labels $20) x126

Pre-Printed Bar Code Labels – (Set of 1,000 labels $30) x145

Additional ISBN assignments – (1st ISBN $55, additional $40 each) x240

The Library of Congress : Preassigned Control Number - http://pcn.loc.gov/

To view a listing of common FAQ's - http://pcn.loc.gov/pcnfaq.html#control

Amazon Advantage Program – www.amazon.com (click here for direct link)

Publishers Marketing Association (PMA) – www.pma-online.org

POZAN

By John Clark

"I found it to be a fascinating account which stays close to what I know took place (as based upon our meetings over the years). John Clark is a brave and inquisitive man who has not only had a long series of bizarre personal encounters but has rejected the evil side for the good. His quest for closure and understanding is a model for many others."

Dr. Richard Haines
Retired NASA Scientist

"Great story. I find John Clark,s work most fascinating. What he reports is consonant with my findings with other subjects."

Dr. James A. Harder
Professor U. C. Berkeley.

"Pozan is eerily powerful."

Peter Brimelow
Senior Editor Forbes Magazine.

"A weird and wild ride that draws you in deeper and deeper as you gradually leave behind the known world and approach the supernatural. I tried to tell myself that this stuff only happens in the movies. That says it all."

Tim Randall
Georgetown University.

"A real page turner."

Cliff Garcia

14359053R00069